AROUND
SCOTLAND'S SHORES

VICTORIANS AND EDWARDIANS IN COLOUR

JOHN HANNAVY

First published in paperback in Great Britain in 2009 by

GW Publishing,
PO Box 6091, Thatcham, Berkshire, RG19 8XZ
Tel + 44 (0)1635 268080
www.gwpublishing.com

ISBN 978-0-9561211-1-0

Printing - Printer Trento, Italy

previous page: *Crewmen on a Clyde tugboat, c.1908, watch an unidentified paddle steamer pulling away from Glasgow's Broomielaw, while crowds wait on the quayside to board another steamer.*

above: *A group of men stand in front of the Royal Arch at Dundee Docks, c.1910. The arch was completed 'in the Norman style' at a cost of over £2000 in 1848 to commemorate a visit by Queen Victoria in 1844 – the first visit to the city by a reigning monarch for nearly 200 years! It survived until demolition in 1964 to make way for the approach roads for the Tay Road Bridge, the masonry being ignominiously dumped in the redundant Earl Grey Dock to serve as the foundations for further work associated with the bridge.*

left: *The herring fishing industry once employed tens of thousands of men and women around Scotland's coast – catching, landing, gutting and selling the fish – with thousands of others involved in essential support industries such as barrel-making, transport, net-making, boat-building and boat repair.*

CONTENTS

above: Two young women carrying peat home to Stornoway c.1903. This postcard was mailed in early 1905 to 'Miss Lloyd' at an address in Clitheroe in Lancashire. The sender noted that "This is the style of most of the girls around the port. We are having a jolly time, weather favouring us – walking, driving, cycling, fishing – the time is flying away like a flash".

INTRODUCTION

above: The children's paddling ponds at Gourock, c.1907, with all the children dressed as if for a formal party (or even Sunday School) rather than a romp in the sea. Easy railway access from Glasgow had helped make Gourock a very popular seaside resort by the second half of the 19th century. At the time this picture was taken, as an addition to its existing shallow paddling pools, Edwardian Gourock was building a fine new tidal swimming pool which opened in 1909.

It is a little over a century and a half since photography first became able to capture a picture of Victorian life – or at least those activities which could endure the long exposure required by early paper negatives. Early Scottish photography is a priceless archive of inspiration and information. Scottish photographers were at the forefront of innovation as the medium was developed and their subject matter was wide-ranging, drawn from Scotland's rugged landscape, historic buildings and people.

Scotland's coast, understandably, was a rich source of subject matter, and throughout the 19th century Scottish photographers sought to record and interpret the lifestyle of those who lived along the country's long and rugged shoreline.

As the century progressed – and the number of photographers increased and exposure times reduced – the variety of imagery ranged from the simply descriptive to the creative and imaginative.

Alongside the growth of photography (and feeding it) was the expansion of the railway network, the development of the tourist industry and the introduction of statutory holidays.

By the dawn of the picture postcard era, Scotland was riding the crest of an industrial and commercial wave, and nowhere was this more apparent than along the coast.

Shipbuilding, import and export, fishing and a variety of other industries were all enjoying commercial success. It is hardly surprising that the emerging picture postcard companies sought to exploit these industries as subjects for their cards.

Despite only being a century old, many of the illustrations in this book seem to show a world as completely different to our own as might be possible. This was a simpler time and a harder time: a richer time for some and a poorer time for most. But above all it was a time when the picture postcard reigned supreme. It was the text messaging system of its time, when several postal collections and deliveries daily made it quite a normal practice to use the Royal Mail to check arrangements with a friend for a planned meeting later that same day.

The idea for this book has been with me for several years, ever since I added a fascination for the richness and variety of Edwardian postcards to my long-standing enthusiasm for Victorian and Edwardian photography.

This book is about a virtual journey from the Solway in Scotland's southwest to the border just north of Berwick-on-Tweed. It is a journey which covers almost a thousand miles, spanning about 50 years (embracing the period 1860–1910), and illustrates a period when Scotland was somewhat disparagingly referred to by officialdom as 'North Britain'.

It covers the years when the legacy of Queen Victoria's love affair with the Scottish Highlands was still being felt and when Sir Walter Scott's romantic recreations of Scotland's clan history still sold in their tens of thousands. But of Scotland's coast and the life and work of those who lived there, little was known south of the border.

Given the blandness of today's picture postcards, early 20th century cards are a revelation. They are rich in historical information (fashions, means of transport, lifestyles, etc.), in fact everything that today's cards are not. The economics of card production these days dictates that the card must be devoid of as much dating material as possible in order to ensure a long shelf life. The rapid and high turnover of cards a century ago meant that exactly the opposite philosophy prevailed.

If the postcard was to succeed as the everyday means of communication, then it had to be attractive, interesting, inexpensive, relevant and reliable. The early postcard publishers ensured it was all those things.

High-quality photography, carefully hand-coloured and then printed (often in Saxony) using the latest lithographic techniques, created a highly attractive product which went far beyond being a simple means of communication.

What better way could there be to popularise the picture postcard than to use pictures of identifiable people? So Edwardian cards show us people at work, people at play, people getting on and off ferries, trains and coaches and holiday resorts crowded to bursting point. In so doing, they offer us more than a simple snapshot of what life was really like in the years before the Great War. How many of those crowding the decks of a pleasure steamer in Leith Docks would have bought copies of the postcard on which they were so clearly visible? Ferry passengers would doubtless enjoy the fact that they could communicate with their friends using cards in which they and their friends could be seen disembarking at Newport on Tay or Dundee.

Compiling a book like this is, of course, dependent upon available material. If Victorian and Edwardian travellers did not visit a location in significant numbers, then there was no commercial imperative to produce photographs or postcards, and certainly little or no incentive to produce them in colour. Many now-popular parts of Scotland remained relatively inaccessible to tourists until the expansion of road-building and the establishment of improved transport networks after the Great War.

John Hannavy, 2009

above: Posing for the camera was a popular pastime and being recognised in postcards probably helped sales! This scene was photographed in Leith's Tolbooth Wynd

below: Kirkcaldy's skyline left the visitor in no doubt it was an industrial town as well as a holiday resort.

NEWHAVEN FISHWIFE

D Macara   *Edinburgh.*

above: *A carte-de-visite studio portrait of a Newhaven fishwife, by D Macara of Edinburgh, c.1870. Fisherwomen earned a small fee for posing for local photographers.*

right: *A coloured postcard of a later generation of Newhaven Fishwives c.1905, photographed by Alex Inglis, successor to Hill and Adamson, at his Calton Hill studio in Edinburgh.*

KIRKCUDBRIGHT

To stand on the quay at Kirkcudbright at low tide today, the visitor would find it difficult to believe that quite large ships regularly used the harbour for more than two centuries.

When Daniel Defoe visited Kirkcudbright in 1720, however, he noted that here was "a harbour without ships, a port without trade, a fishery without nets". By the middle of the 19th century things had improved considerably. Trade with Ireland had been revitalised, a fishing fleet was based in the harbour and prosperity had returned.

The harbour in this picture is no more, long since filled in to make way for car parking, but the town retains much of its 18th and 19th century charm.

A mecca for artists a century ago, Kirkcudbright had a thriving artists' colony from the closing years of the 19th century well into the 1930s. Today, it is a quiet but very attractive backwater.

above: *This beautiful view of Kirkcudbright Harbour was taken in the 1890s but not published as a Valentine postcard until 1903, by which time both of the ships shown here had been lost at sea.*

STRANRAER

left: Stranraer from the West Pier, seen in a postcard from 1904. Miss Cathcart in County Antrim received this card from her friend "M.M." who would have arrived by steamer from Larne. M.M. wrote "Sorry you cannot be here. I have a notion to remain myself".

To most people, the little port of Stranraer is synonymous with travelling to Ireland. Ferries have set out from the Loch Ryan port for Larne in Northern Ireland for over 180 years.

The town built the first pier specifically for the Irish ferry trade in 1820, and a second pier was completed 20 years later. By the 1850s those two projects, coupled with Stranraer's position in a natural safe harbour, effectively stole the ferry business from Portpatrick a few miles away on the more exposed west coast of Galloway. Portpatrick had been the point of departure for services to Ireland for 200 years.

On the other side of the Irish Sea, the establishment of a railway line from Carrickfergus to Larne at the same time made Larne the obvious choice for the Irish end of the service, rather than Donaghdee which had been served from Portpatrick.

The 1850s saw the introduction of the paddle steamer Briton on the Stranraer–Larne service and the establishment of a daily timetable, but the service never made a profit and was withdrawn in 1863.

Eight years later, the establishment of the Larne and Stranraer Steamboat Company reintroduced the service, with the paddle steamer *Princess Louise* (the first of many 'princesses' on the route) doing the daily crossing.

The ferry service is now under threat as carriers move their operations to Cairnryan to take advantage of the shorter crossing to Ireland. P&O moved 30 years ago, and Stena will now follow.

above: Stranraer Pier c.1909. The vessel is probably the PS Princess May. At just over 1200 tons, this was the slightly larger of the two paddle steamers which regularly made the crossing to Ireland. She and her smaller sister, the PS Princess Victoria, were the last two paddle steamers to serve the route. It has long been a tradition for the ships on the Stranraer–Larne crossing to be named 'Princesses' – a tradition which was continued until relatively recently.

BALLANTRAE

In name at least, the little Ayrshire village of Ballantrae (13 miles south of Girvan at the mouth of the wonderfully named River Stinchar) will be forever associated with Robert Louis Stevenson's novel *The Master of Ballantrae*.

In fact, the book was not set there at all. Stevenson simply liked the lyrical rhythm of the phrase 'The Master of Ballantrae' which had come to him while staying in the village in 1876. His wife later wrote in the preface to the book: "for years the title lay dormant in his mind". It was 5 years before he even started work on the story, and 13 before it was published! Despite the tranquil scene captured in the 1908 postcard, below, fishing was the mainstay of village life 100 years ago. Even today, the harbour hosts a small number of crab and lobster boats. It is on the tourist trade that the village now depends, however.

GIRVAN

Girvan, located 30 miles north of Stranraer and 20 miles south of Ayr, has had a varied and distinguished history dating from its establishment as a Burgh in the closing years of the 17th century.

By the middle of the 19th century, with the Scottish herring industry in its ascendancy, Girvan was well established as a fishing and trading port with a substantial fishing fleet, weekly fish markets, a thriving coastal trade and a growing trade with Ireland.

Briefly, in the mid 19th century, Girvan harbour was one of the many Scottish departure points for hundreds of emigrants bound for Canada. By the 1880s, with both the coastal trade and export trade booming, a new pier and breakwater were completed to handle the increased shipping.

Reflecting the growth in shipping traffic in and out of the harbour, Girvan's first lifeboat – the *Earl of Carrick* – was stationed in the town in 1865, initiating a tradition which continues today.

Girvan's history as a tourist resort dates from 1860, with the arrival of the branch railway from Maybole and the establishment of coastal steamer services from Glasgow and Ayr. There were plans to establish a steam packet route between Girvan and Ireland, but they never came to fruition.

With the opening of the Girvan and Portpatrick Junction Railway in 1877, the development of Portpatrick as the ferry port was ensured. Girvan, however, continued to exploit its fine beaches and other tourist amenities and by 1900 the influx of tourists trebled the town's population during the summer.

above right: Dalrymple Street, Girvan, c.1905, with a three-horse charabanc laden with tourists approaching the camera. To the left of the carriage, the premises of 'P Ross, Flesher' appear to be closed while Mrs J Wilson has drawn the blinds to protect her confectionery from the sun. The octagonal tower is the McKechnie Institute, completed in 1888 as a local subscription library and reading room, funded by a bequest from the estate of a Girvan grocer. It has since been used for a variety of purposes, including social and educational centre, library and, since 1982, local history museum and exhibition venue.

right: A quiet day in Girvan Harbour, photographed c.1908.

AYR

right: An interesting mixture of steam and sail in Ayr Harbour, c.1905. The harbour, which had for centuries lined both sides of the River Ayr, was extended in the 19th century. An enclosed dock sited to the north of the river, importing a wide range of goods and handling coal and other exports, was constructed.

below: The paddle steamer Neptune entering Ayr Harbour in 1906. The pier, left, was a popular promenade for local people and visitors, affording great views of the traffic in and out of the harbour. The Neptune was completed in 1892 by Napier, Shanks and Bell. After 4 years working as a ferry on various Clyde services, she served as a cruise ship until the outbreak of the Great War. She was then requisitioned as a minesweeper and renamed HMS Nepaulin. She was mined and sunk in April 1917.

below right: The PS Juno off Ayr, c.1904. Juno was built in 1898 by the Clydebank Engineering and Shipbuilding Company, and based at Ayr. The 600 ton steamer served as a cruise ship for excursions from Ayr until the outbreak of the Great War, when she was renamed HMS Junior and operated as a minesweeper in the Firth of Forth. She returned to Ayr in 1919, worked there for a further 12 years, and was eventually broken up at Alloa Docks in 1932.

Ayr on the Firth of Clyde successfully combined the twin challenges of being a successful seaport and one of the west coast's best holiday resorts.

In the 18th century, the harbour was the point of entry for cargoes of tobacco, and used to export coal, timber and a range of general goods. Timber is still shipped out of Scotland from Ayr Docks today, an export which is actually increasing.

Sited on the River Ayr, where it enters the Firth of Clyde, the town's harbour always suffered from the considerable tidal rise and fall. This limited access to a few hours either side of high tide. Considerable dredging was required as ships got bigger, prompting the construction of deeper water docks in the 19th century.

A popular centre for horse-racing since the 18th century, the Ayr Gold Cup was first run in 1805. The racecourse was moved to its present site in 1907 and is, today, Scotland's only Grade One racecourse.

TROON

inset below: Troon from the rocks, a 1907 postcard published by Valentines of Dundee. "Playing golf once or twice a day" wrote Logan to his friend Master W Shanks in Hamilton.

In the opening years of the 19th century, Troon was a little coastal village consisting of just a few cottages.

With the development of the Ayrshire coalfields, the building of a new harbour and the arrival of the first industrial railway in Scotland (the Duke of Portland's horse-drawn railway opened in 1812), coal began to be shipped out of Troon in increasing quantities.

By the middle of the century over 170,000 tons of coal was being shipped out through the docks, a great deal of it to Ireland. The railway was not licensed to carry passengers, but this minor technicality was circumvented by weighing passengers and costing their transport as if they were freight!

By 1840, the expanding town had a direct passenger rail link with Glasgow. Like so many other small towns and villages along the Ayrshire and Firth of Clyde coasts, Troon started to enjoy increasing popularity as a holiday resort.

Blessed with miles of beautiful beaches, the town quickly became very popular and a whole new industry in tourist lodgings grew up along the seafront.

Troon is perhaps best known today for its challenging links golf courses. Golf was first

offered as one of its visitor attractions in 1878 (27 years after nearby Prestwick) with the opening of a five-hole course, expanded to a full eighteen-hole 8 years later. Just a few years after the time frame of this book, it hosted the Open for the first time in 1923. Now almost completely surrounded by golf courses, the town claims that more golf is played in Troon than anywhere else in Scotland!

Today, the coal fields and the shipping trade are both long gone – the harbour is now a popular marina – but the contact with Ireland survives in the form of a regular Supercat ferry service from the port.

main picture: A busy scene on one of Troon's fine beaches, photographed in the summer of 1902. An ice-cream barrow is open for business on the left, while groups of children enjoy themselves along the shore in the centre. Interestingly, the photographer must actually have been in the water to take this picture!

SALTCOATS

As its name might suggest, salt played a major part in the history of this little Ayrshire town. The tradition of salt-making can be traced back to before the 16th century. Although some salt panning took place on the coast, most of the salt was not dried in pans but produced by boiling sea water – using the readily available supply of locally mined coal as the heat source.

Exporting Ayrshire coal to Ireland provided a significant source of income for the town from the late 17th century. Coal was therefore one of the driving forces behind the development of the harbour, with forty vessels used on the trade by 1837. Another significant local source of employment was the textile industry, with a considerable number of muslin weavers working in the town and selling their wares in Paisley and Glasgow. It was after the arrival of the railway in the 1840s that the town started to become a popular holiday resort; even in the mid 19th century it was less than an hour's journey from Glasgow.

top: Eglinton Street, Saltcoats, from a postcard sent to an address in Portland, Maine, in August 1908 by an American family enjoying a short holiday in what they describe as a "nice seaside place with fine weather". This style of housing is typical of a number of Ayrshire villages.

above: The Beach and Esplanade in summer, Saltcoats, photographed c.1908. By the time this card was published, Saltcoats was one of the most popular summer holiday destinations for families from Scotland's industrial heartland.

right: On the Esplanade, Saltcoats, 1902. This beautiful early Edwardian scene is from a postcard published in London and printed in Dresden. The crowds are probably watching a Pierrot group perform on a makeshift stage on the beach – a popular holiday entertainment in towns all around the coast.

ARDROSSAN

When Thomas Cook, the pioneer of the package holiday, brought his first ever group of visitors to Scotland in 1846 (a temperance group from England), the party sailed to Ardrossan from Fleetwood on the Lancashire Coast as the cross-border railway line had not yet been laid. Ardrossan harbour was their first landfall in Scotland.

The building of a large harbour had originally been proposed at the end of the 18th century and none other than Thomas Telford surveyed the coast in the early 1800s. It took a further 50 years before the harbour was completed, but by that time it offered regular sailings to Arran (introduced in 1834) as well as England. The Arran service, now operated by Caledonian MacBrayne, continues today.

Shipbuilding dominated local industry throughout much of the Victorian and Edwardian eras, with some of the largest wooden-hulled vessels ever built in Scotland being launched from Ardrossan yards.

above: Passengers embarking on two of the many steamers to use Ardrossan. The 600 ton turbine steamer Duchess of Argyll *(right) was built in 1906 by William Denny for the Arran run. The 1700 ton turbine steamer* Viper *(left), built by Fairfields of Govan also in 1906, was used on the daytime Belfast crossing.*

GREAT CUMBRAE

right: Millport's East Bay, captured by a postcard photographer c.1905, depicts the pleasures of a simple seaside holiday.

below: Boating in Kames Bay, from a postcard mailed from Millport in August 1905. "We are enjoying ourselves well, it is a pretty place" wrote 'MB' to her friend Miss Ballantyne, but noted "this is an awful stylish place this, and everything is very high price!" MB was staying in the large white guest house at the left of the view, so perhaps it was the guest house rather than Millport to which she was referring.

The Reverend James Adams, an early 19th century minister at the little church on Great Cumbrae, is remembered for a prayer in which he asked God to bless the Cumbrae islands and to bestow his blessings on "the adjacent islands of Great Britain and Ireland"!

In 1876, Butterfield's Victorian Gothic Episcopal 'Cathedral of the Isles' was completed in Millport and, with only 100 seats, is celebrated as the smallest cathedral in Britain.

The Cumbraes (which, along with Bute and Arran, made up the old county of Buteshire) grew in popularity in the late 19th and early 20th centuries as both holiday and day-trip destinations for visitors from those 'adjacent islands'. The visitors crossed from Largs to Great Cumbrae on one of the many Clyde ferries. While never as busy as their larger neighbours, the Cumbraes enjoyed a popularity in Victorian and Edwardian times which belied their size. They are much quieter today!

LARGS

left: The Slip, Largs Bay, c.1903, a Reliable Series postcard mailed by a holidaymaker to an address in Formby, Lancashire in 1904.

below: The Pier Head and the Eglinton Temperance Hotel, Largs, c.1909. Temperance hotels were enjoying significant popularity at the time, as were 'dry boats', steamers on which no alcohol was served. Mothers preferred such boats and hotels as holiday destinations, as they kept dad out of the pub for a few days!

Despite the fact that the railway line from Glasgow did not reach Largs until late in the 19th century (in fact, the Glasgow and South Western Railway only opened in the mid-1880s), Largs was developing as a holiday resort from the early years of the century. The coach journey from Glasgow could take two full days at that time! The alternative was a long ferry journey down the Clyde from Glasgow. With the railway, however, the journey was less than an hour and the town's expansion was rapid. Before then, like so many other towns along this stretch of the west coast, fishing and weaving were the most significant employers.

The railway brought with it as many trainloads of tourists intent on passing through the town as staying there, as the trains connected with boats from Fairlie Pier to Arran and Cumbrae.

Ferries still operate from Largs today, as the main connection between the mainland and northern tip of Great Cumbrae.

Wemyss Bay's Pier and the new Railway Station, built by the Caledonian Railway in 1903. At the pier, the Rothesay boat is preparing for departure. The paddle steamer is probably either the 244 ton PS Caledonia built in 1889 or the 246 ton PS Marchioness of Breadalbane completed the following year. Both boats regularly worked the Wemyss Bay to Rothesay service. *Marchioness of*

CALEDONIAN RAILWAY

Breadalbane *remained in service for 47 years, while Caledonia was scrapped in 1933. Both vessels were built at Reid's shipyard in Port Glasgow. This beautifully printed postcard – manufactured in Saxony – was probably published to celebrate the completion of the new station*

WEMYSS BAY

above: The 331 ton paddle steamer Galatea, *built by Cairds in Greenock in 1889 for the Caledonian Steam Packet Company, brought sightseers from several of the resorts on Bute to watch the great fireworks display organised for the company at Wemyss Bay by Brocks on August 22nd 1890. She was sold in 1906.*

below: The great explorer David Livingstone was a regular visitor to Kelly House, Wemyss Bay. After his death, a replica of his African hut was built in the grounds in 1875 and became a local landmark.

When the railway arrived in Wemyss Bay in 1865, it heralded a period of considerable development. It brought thousands of tourists en route to Rothesay, and just as many looking for a holiday in the town itself.

The station as completed in the 1860s by the Wemyss Bay Railway Company was a much simpler affair than that which survives today. James Millar's splendid steel and glass structure, with its famous circular Booking Office and John Menzies bookstall, has been the subject of dozens of postcards since it was completed for the Caledonian Railway Company in 1903.

The sheer size of the booking hall and the width of the covered walkway to the pier give some idea of the scale of the seasonal passenger traffic which used the rail and steamer service.

To many, Wemyss Bay was little more than a brief stop between train and steamer. However, to those who lived and worked on the Isle of Bute, it was the commercial lifeline which sustained their tourist industry.

On 22nd August 1890, the Caledonian Steam Packet Company organised "The Most MAGNIFICENT DISPLAY of FIREWORKS EVER EXHIBITED IN SCOTLAND" at Wemyss Bay, and used numerous steamers to bring spectators from all along the Clyde. For a shilling a head for the round trip, passengers from Gourock, Helensburgh, Kirn, Dunoon, Innellan, Kilcreggan, Hunters Quay, Rothesay, Largs, Millport, Whiting Bay, Lamlash, King's Cross, Brodick, Corrie and all piers along the way were brought to vantage points just offshore. The sight of at least seven paddle steamers crowded with sightseers all moored together in the river must have been almost as impressive as Messrs Brock and Company's firework display, which included "Jewelled Clouds, Flights of Rockets, Shooting Stars" and "a Host of Brilliant Pyrotechnic Devices"!

David Livingstone, Anthony Trollope and other notable figures have visited the town, but few reminders of them survive. Even Castle Wemyss, where Anthony Trollope wrote part of his novel *Barchester Towers*, was demolished in the 1980s.

GOUROCK

right: An unidentified steamer leaving Gourock Pier c.1906. The unusually large paddle-boxes suggest it might be the PS Edinburgh Castle, *leaving on her regular summer sailing to Lochgoilhead*

below: The Parade, Gourock, from a Valentine's postcard, c.1909.

Gourock was originally established as a fishing village in times when herring were plentiful in the Firth of Clyde. However, by the late 18th century the fishing industry had long since diminished and the small town was reinventing itself both as an industrial centre and as a tourist resort. The Gourock Ropework Company was based in the town from the 1730s until it moved to Port Glasgow in the 1850s, and copper mining was started just outside the town in the 1780s. Textiles were also made in Gourock from the late 18th century.

By the early 19th century, the town was becoming a popular tourist destination for people from Glasgow. The first steamboat service to the town (the famous *SS Comet*) can be traced back to 1812. By the end of the century, with railway services from Glasgow direct to the pierhead, Gourock was the starting point for many a journey 'doon the watter' on the dozens of steamers which visited the town. The steamer services survived into the 1960s, but only the Clyde ferries remain today.

GREENOCK

right: Not a car in sight in this busy scene in Cathcart Street Greenock, 1906, from the 'Reliable Series' of postcards.

below: The paddle steamer Minerva built in 1893, 306 gross tonnage, at Greenock's Princes Pier in 1906. The steamer, built at Clydebank by J and G Thomson, sailed the Clyde until she was broken up in 1927. In her 24 years of working life on the river, she was used on several regular year-round routes from Ardrossan with spells of summer cruising 'doon the watter' before seeing wartime service based in Malta. She was captured by the Turkish navy in 1917 and, despite being returned after the war ended, was eventually sold to a Turkish owner, seeing out her working life as a ferry on the Bosphorous.

Situated around a bay, protected by the end of a long sandbank 21 miles sailing from Glasgow, Greenock has long been referred to by those on the river as the 'tail of the bank'.

The port dates back to the 17th century when it was one of Scotland's busiest herring ports. With approaching a thousand boats using the harbour, Greenock's boats rivalled the great herring fleets of the east coast.

By the 19th century, however, import and export trade was replacing fishing. By the middle of the century, and with a much-expanded harbour, Greenock was recognised as the country's most important port.

In trade directories for the 1830s, the diversity of the town's industry is evident. Listings include two engine works, six sugar refineries, a number of rope works, three foundries, three tanneries, three breweries, two potteries and a distillery. As well

as these there were manufacturers of glass, cloth, sailcloth, soap, candles, flax and paper. With seven harbours and over four miles of quays, Greenock could handle a huge volume of traffic.

With such a thriving shipping industry, it is no surprise that the town expanded into ship-building. By the early years of the 19th century, it was one of the largest centres of shipbuilding in the country with no fewer than six shipyards operational in the 1830s. Many fine and famous vessels were launched from Greenock yards, among them several great liners for Cunard and P&O. Passenger ships plied between Greenock and Ireland and to several ports along Scotland's west coast.

When the tourist trade started to expand, many of the Clyde paddle steamers were based in the harbour. The services to Dunoon and elsewhere embarked from Princes Pier, the largest quay in the town.

As well as its legacy as once having been the busiest port on the Clyde, exporting machinery and importing sugar and general goods, Greenock is famous as the birthplace of James Watt. The father of the steam engine, James Watt was arguably the

above: Greenock's West Quay with Clyde steamers lined up as far as the eye can see. At least seven are visible in this superb postcard from c.1905.

inventor whose genius fuelled both the Industrial Revolution and the success of the Clyde as the home of shipbuilding. Named after the inventor, the huge two thousand foot long James Watt Dock was completed in 1886 after 7 years construction.

To further underline his association with the town, Greenock also has a James Watt College, a school named after him and the Watt Museum and Library. The Museum and Library were originally opened in 1837 by Watt's son as the Watt Institution, containing a library and a fine marble statue of the inventor himself.

Greenock may also have been the birthplace of the famous pirate Captain William Kidd, but it is for fishing, whaling and its dominance of trade with the rest of the world rather than piracy that the town earned its real fame.

Today its importance as a cornerstone of Scotland's maritime industry is little more than a memory, but Clyde steamers still serve the quays as they have done for more than a century and a half.

As an important and strategic port, Greenock was heavily bombed in World War II. It was, for a time, the wartime base of the Free French.

This busy view of Princes Quay with passengers making their way to an unidentified steamer was published in 1902. On the back of the card (sent to Miss Walker in Lytham St Annes in Lancashire) JDW holidaying in Rothesay wrote "This is where we came to by train, thence one and a half hours sail here where we are very comfortable - good rooms and a splendid view."

PORT GLASGOW

above: Unusually, this postcard ignores the river from which Port Glasgow derived its wealth, and concentrates on the railway station with its plethora of advertisements for, among other things, whisky, soap, tobacco, sausages, coffee and Nestlé's Milk. The railway arrived in the town in the early 1840s, some 60 years before this photograph was taken.

Before the end of the 17th century, Port Glasgow did not exist. Twenty miles from Glasgow, the port was created in the 1690s as New-Port Glasgow, the closest point to the city which could be reached by the largest ships of the day.

Continuous dredging in the centuries which followed ensured that ever-larger ships could be sailed ever further up river and into the city itself.

By the early years of the 19th century, the importance of Port Glasgow was considerable. In 1812, the burgh's place in maritime history was assured when Henry Bell's pioneering steamship *Comet* was launched. Built at John Wood's Port Glasgow shipyard, *Comet* was the first steam-powered ship on the river and indeed the first in Europe. From those small beginnings grew all the Clyde's steamship building legacy.

The railway reached Port Glasgow in the early 1840s when the Glasgow, Paisley and Greenock Railway opened. By that time the town's importance as a port had declined, but as a centre for shipbuilding it was very definitely in the ascendancy. Yards such as Lithgow's were at the forefront of steamship design and build.

CLYDEBANK

above: The Cunarder RMS Caronia *on the stocks at John Brown's yard in 1904.*

below: This 1904 view of the Singer Sewing Machine factory shows a large proportion of the 5000-strong workforce. The factory, built by Robert McAlpine, opened in 1884. Over the following 60 years it turned out over 23 million sewing machines!

above: Glasgow Road, Clydebank with the entrance to the world famous John Brown's Shipyards, from where some of the most famous ships in the world were launched, on the left. Browns was one of the town's major employers well into the middle of the 20th century.

The name of Clydebank is synonymous with shipbuilding, and especially with the world famous shipyard of John Brown and Company where many of the finest Cunard liners were built.

The shipyard which became famous as John Brown's was established as long ago as 1851 at Bankton near Govan as J and G Thomson, and their first ship was launched in the following year. They moved to a new 32 acre site at Barns of Clyde near Dalmuir in 1871, in the area which later became known as Clydebank.

John Brown, a Sheffield steel-maker, took the yard over in 1899 when it was known as the Clydebank Shipbuilding and Engineering Company. It entered its golden age under Brown's management, thanks in no small part to the innovative engines it developed in conjunction with the American Curtis Marine Turbine Company.

Even at the dawn of the 20th century, the scale of some of the vessels being built there was awesome. The twin-funnelled, 19,500 ton *RMS Caronia*, seen above left on the stocks at John Brown's yard, was over 670 feet in length. When she entered service in 1905, she regularly plied between Liverpool and New York carrying over 1500 passengers. This view

of the ship was taken shortly before her launch on July 13th 1904. The ship was one of the first Cunarders to be used as a cruise-ship from 1906, regularly carrying parties of Americans from New York on tours around the Mediterranean countries and helping establish a completely new type of holiday experience.

The nature of the river at Clydebank, where the River Cart flowed into the Clyde, made it an ideal location for launching large ships. As *Caronia* was being prepared for launch, the keel of the 780 foot long, 44,000 ton *RMS Lusitania* was being laid in the same yard.

Other larger ships followed, culminating in the great 'Queens' in the 1930s and of course Cunard's iconic *QEII* in the 1960s. The company's first Cunarder, the 2,241 ton *Jura*, had been launched by J and G Thomson over a century earlier in 1854. The yard closed in 1972 after 101 years at Clydebank.

above: Despite the importance of shipbuilding on the Clyde in Edwardian times, postcards of the shipyards were not produced in any great numbers. This 1908 view of John Brown's yard with a large ship in the stocks is therefore a rarity.

right: John Brown's yard was not only famous for building large passenger ships – the company also carried out extensive work for the Royal Navy. When the keel for HMS Sutlej was laid down in 1898, a 12,000 ton Cressy Class cruiser, the yard was trading as the Clydebank Engineering and Shipbuilding Company. In the closing years of the 19th century, the yard signed orders for four cruisers and seven destroyers for the Royal Navy (including one of HMS Sutlez's sister ships HMS Bacchante) as well as warships for the navies of Spain, Japan and Russia. This photograph of HMS Sutlez is believed to have been taken during her sea trials on the Clyde in 1901 or 1902.

GLASGOW

Although not strictly on the coast, Glasgow's history as the most important port in Scotland demands its inclusion in this tour of the coastline.

From its emergence as an industrial and mercantile town in the middle of the 17th century (the first quay at the Broomielaw is believed to have been built in 1662) Glasgow grew and grew. A deep-sea port was being developed at Port Glasgow before the end of that century, by which time expanding overseas trade in sugar, linen and tobacco, imported from the Americas and the West Indies, was being developed.

With increased trade came increased prosperity and, by the late 1820s, the city's buildings were reflecting its importance. No lesser person than Daniel Defoe in his *Tour through the Whole Island of Great Britain* described it as 'the cleanest and beautifullest and best-built city in Britain' – London excepted, of course!

At the end of the 18th century, Glasgow's

above: Prince's Dock, Glasgow, from a postcard mailed on 7th August 1905. "We arrived here yesterday from Liverpool" wrote the sender "to load for Algiers. We leave on Wednesday". Princes Dock – known as Cessnock Dock before its Royal opening – was opened on September 10th 1897 by the Duke and Duchess of York.

31

top: *This 1905 postcard entitled 'Glasgow Bridge' offers a fine view of the city's open topped electric trams, introduced in 1898. The electric trams replaced horse-drawn vehicles which had been used in the city since 1872.*

above: *A typical summer afternoon in Glasgow's Queen's Park, c.1910, with a crowd gathering for a performance by a large musical ensemble in the bandstand.*

left: *Glasgow's firemen were called into action just after midnight on the morning of 17th August 1909 when an enormous fire, apparently started by a gas explosion, broke out in a block of warehouses in Ingram Street. The explosion and fire demolished an eighty yard stretch of buildings on the north side of Ingram Street, between High Street and Shuttle Street. Such was the interest in the event, that postcards were published by Valentines of Dundee within 48 hours of the fire. This card was posted on August 21st to Miss Galbraith in Herne Hill, London, by her nephew Jack, who had witnessed the fire and believed it was "the biggest one that has ever been in Glasgow". The fire certainly took all night to bring under control and the cost of the damage, estimated at a quarter of a million pounds, was enormous.*

right: Despite its industrial image, life in Edwardian Glasgow wasn't all hard graft as this picture of the tearoom in the Rouken Glen shows. Those enjoying tea, or a bottle of pop, have dressed up in their finery before promenading in the park's well-tended grounds.

below: A paddle steamer pulls away from Glasgow's Broomielaw while passengers embark on the David MacBrayne steamer PS Iona, tied up at the quay. This Valentine postcard, somewhat prosaically entitled 'Off Down the Water, Glasgow' rather than the usual 'Doon the Watter', was produced c.1906. At the time this postcard was produced, Iona (built by J and G Thomson) had already been in service on the river for over 40 years.

population was 50,000 (nearly five times what it had been a century before) and by the end of the 19th century, it would have risen to three quarters of a million. And those people migrated to the city because of the abundance of jobs, none more important than the Clyde's worldwide reputation as the major shipbuilding river in Scotland. 'Clyde-built' came to mean quality and reliability. From less than 20,000 tons of shipping launched into the river in the middle of the 19th century, Clyde shipyards had driven their annual tonnage up to half a million by the time King Edward VII came to the throne in 1901. Within the new King's reign, that figure would increase by half as much again, employing (directly and indirectly) a total in excess of 80,000 people in the first decade of the 20th century.

To house the city's growing population in the 19th century, housing developments went up across the city with tall tenement buildings packed so close together that in many places sunlight never

penetrated as far as ground level! The American Nathaniel Hawthorne wrote in 1856 that conditions in Glasgow epitomised "all that makes city poverty disgusting". In response to a growing public outcry, the Glasgow City Improvement Act was passed in 1868 and a board of Trustees established to oversee the wholesale redevelopment of what were considered to be the worst slums in Europe.

The passing of the act had two immediate effects: the first was a glimmer of hope for the city's poor and the second was the appointment of Glasgow photographer Thomas Annan to produce a photographic record of the prevailing housing conditions. Taken over a period of 9 years, Annan's photographs were intended to contrast with the hugely improved living conditions which would prevail in the rebuilt areas. However, by the 1950s, much of that new housing had once again become awful slums. In human terms, Victorian Glasgow's prosperity always came at a price.

HELENSBURGH

right: The contrast between 'now' and 'then' is so clear when looking at pictures from a century ago. Promenading on Helensburgh Esplanade c.1903 was obviously an event subject to a strict dress code, in vivid contrast to today's casual styles.

below: Taken 2 years later in 1905, this view shows several of the waterfront shops and the Eagle Temperance Hotel – almost every holiday resort in Scotland had one!

With the history and development of the Clyde resorts and industrial towns so inextricably linked with steamships, it is satisfying to reflect that their development was greatly assisted by the decision of Henry Bell and his wife to move to Helensburgh in the opening years of the 19th century.

Bell's pioneering ship the *SS Comet*, Britain's (indeed Europe's) first passenger-carrying steamer, was launched on the Clyde in 1812. The rest is, as they say, history. A monument to him stands by the pier which he also built, as he saw the steamer service as a means of bringing visitors to the hotel he ran with his wife. She was also superintendant of the town's public baths.

Helensburgh's history really only dates from the second half of the 18th century, and for the first 70 years it remained a very small town. It was the arrival of the Glasgow Dumbarton and Helensburgh Railway in 1858 which propelled it into becoming a popular holiday resort for people from Glasgow, as an easily accessible place from which to take ferries 'doon the watter'.

above: Promenading along Helensburgh's waterfront c.1905. A single horse-drawn wagon is parked outside one of the shops. The absence of other traffic obviously gave holidaymakers confidence to walk in the road.

left: Children paddling in the water at Helensburgh, c.1903. In early Edwardian times, beach attire was rather formal. The clothes these children are wearing look more appropriate for Sunday School than the beach!

GARELOCHHEAD

The relentless advance of tourism in Victorian and Edwardian Scotland was not without its problems. One of the more famous incidents of locals trying to stem the advancing tide was the so-called Battle of Garelochhead in 1853.

A regular steamer service to the pier was already well established when the steamer company tried to introduce Sunday sailings. This was anathema to the local landowners who rallied the villagers to blockade the pier and stop the passengers getting ashore from the paddle steamer *Conqueror*.

The tourists won initially, but their success proved to be short-lived as Sunday sailings were quickly abandoned and did not return for many years.

By the time these postcards were produced, visitors had a wide choice of transport. There were of course the steamers and motor omnibuses and, from 1894, a direct railway link with Glasgow.

Today the Gare Loch is best known as Britain's nuclear submarine base.

above: The Pier, Garelochhead, c.1906. Two steamers are at the pier; the one nearer the pier head is probably the 1898-built PS Juno, *a regular cruise ship on the Clyde and down as far as Ayr for over 30 years. The pier, originally opened in 1845, had been rebuilt in 1879. It continued in use until closure at the outbreak of the Second World War, and was demolished 53 years later in 1992.*

right: The Garelochhead Hotel, c.1904. Alice, writing to her friend Miss Drabble, reported "Came here by motor this morning, going back by steamer. Glorious day." Given the speed of both motor transport and steamers, she must have been holidaying just a few miles away (perhaps at Helensburgh 7 miles south?) to complete such a round trip in a day.

LOCHGOILHEAD

Before the 1820s, few people would have heard of Lochgoilhead. The head of Loch Goil was largely inaccessible until the advent of a summer steamer service from Greenock, Gourock and Helensburgh opened the area up to visitors.

The Loch Goil and Loch Long Steamboat Company was formed in 1825 initially to establish a route to take travellers to Oban and Inveraray, but the service also opened up this remote and beautiful area of Argyll itself to tourists.

While for many the trip up the loch was a pleasant summer's day out, for others it gave access to a growing number of holiday homes in this once-remote corner. The steamer routes really were the holiday motorways of their day!

After successive takeovers, steamer services to the village finally ceased at the end of the Second World War, by which time road access to the area had been considerably improved.

Today many visitors still spend their summers in the area, which now has a holiday village complex.

above: A group of people enjoying a picnic at Carrick Castle in 1909 pose for the camera against the dramatic backdrop of Loch Goil.

left: Two ferries lie moored at Lochgoilhead pier, one of the most northerly ports of call for the Clyde paddle-steamers. The Loch Goil and Loch Long Steamboat Company employed several steamers on the route from Gourock to Lochgoilhead, the most famous being the 260 ton PS Edinburgh Castle, *built in 1879 and scrapped in 1913. She was the company's biggest and most luxurious vessel. The steamer furthest from the pier in this 1906 view is believed to be the Edinburgh Castle. After 1909, the company was taken over and became the Loch Goil and Inveraray Steamboat Company.*

KIRN

above: The Pleasure Gardens opened to the public in 1904, and were an instant success. This postcard was published to commemorate the opening and offers an unusual view. Giving centre-stage treatment to the African youth with the large parasol is unusual for the period.

In Edwardian times, Kirn was a small resort between Hunter's Quay and Dunoon very much with its own identity; this is despite the fact that the three had been united as a single burgh as early as 1868. It was described as 'a pleasant watering-hole', had its own pier and was regularly served by several Clyde steamer routes.

With beautifully laid out Pleasure Gardens and a profusion of teashops and tea gardens, it catered for the genteel holidaymaker seeking the bracing sea air of the Holy Loch and the Clyde estuary. However,

Ina (who sent the postcard, *above right*, to her friend in Kelvinside) was less than impressed. "Weather very bad again", she wrote, "can't go out today at all." Bessie, however, who sent the postcard of the Pleasure Gardens, *above*, to her friend in Glasgow, did not wish to return home at all, as she was "having spent a most enjoyable holiday" in May 1905.

The New Esplanade was completed in 1893 (a little over a decade before these three photographs were taken) and its completion significantly enhanced the resort's shoreline.

below: The New Esplanade, photographed in 1904. The new esplanade was completed in 1893 to improve what had then been a run down stretch of coastline

right: The West End and Alexandra Parade, showing a fine Victorian water fountain, from a postcard c.1905. As early as 1888, Kirn had been described as 'A fashionable watering place consisting of superior villa residences and neat cottages on the western shore of the Firth between Dunoon and Hunter's Quay, with which places it is virtually one.' The Kirn Pier Company was established in 1846 and, like Dunoon and Hunters Quay, Kirn was a regular stopping place for Clyde steamers. In August 1890, the Caledonian Steam Packet Company's steamer Marchioness of Bute took holidaymakers from Kirn to the great fireworks display at Wemyss Bay.

DUNOON

right: The Esplanade and Pier, Dunoon, c.1908. Dunoon Pier was a port of call for many of the Clyde steamer routes. The extensive wooden pier structure with its buildings was about 20 years old at the time this picture was taken. The 120 year old structure is still in service today.

below: East Bay, Dunoon, c.1902. For reasons lost in the mists of time, East Bay and West Bay are actually north and south of each other!

A settlement on the site of present-day Dunoon has existed for centuries; there has been a village there since mediaeval times. However, it was the pleasure steamer which proved to be the engine of the town's development as a holiday resort.

A regular steamer service to Glasgow was instigated in the 1840s and, with the arrival of the railway at Gourock just across the river, Dunoon's popularity as the gateway to Cowal quickly grew.

By the early 1800s, fine holiday villas were starting to appear along the shoreline. By the end of the 19th century, a substantial town had grown up to cater for the needs of the growing numbers of visitors.

The present wooden pier, a listed structure still used by the side-loading Gourock Ferry today, dates from the late Victorian period. There are plans to replace it with a proposed new linkspan in 2011.

left: Argyle Street, Dunoon, on a busy day in 1905. This postcard was sent by a holidaymaker visiting Dunoon from the east coast in June 1907. "Arrived here [illegible] Left my overcoat on the Leith train at Portobello" he wrote to his friend in Bonnyrigg, "but they have phoned Leith and it is to be sent home." Now that's service!

below left: An alternative view of Dunoon's Esplanade and Pier, c.1905. This was published by Hartmanns who, along with Valentines and the Reliable Series, were the major publishers of tinted postcards of Edwardian Scotland.

below: A large group of people posing outside The West of Scotland Convalescent Home, Dunoon, photographed around 1906 (perhaps on the occasion of a fundraising event?).

right: A view of West Bay, Dunoon, from a 1904 postcard mailed to Durham. The card carries the message "This is one of the Scottish Watering Places known as 'Doon the Watter'".

below: The PS Neptune *off Dunoon in 1905. The 378 ton Neptune was built at Napier's yard in Yoker, and launched in 1892. Working off Dover as a minesweeper during the Great War, she was sunk in 1917.*

below right: Dunoon looking west from the Golf Course, A Valentine's view c.1908.

ISLE OF BUTE

One of many view prints produced by the Photochrom Company of Zurich. Entitled 'Bannatyne, Kyles of Bute', this picture was taken c.1895. The Photochrom Company marketed a series of coloured photographs covering the entire coast of Britain, claiming they were 'real colour photographs'. They were in fact conventional black and white images expertly coloured using lithographic printing.

The village of Port Bannatyne, about a mile from Rothesay, was built around a natural harbour which is still a popular location for yachts. For the Victorian photographer, it offered an idyllic image of the Isle of Bute. Bute, a mere fifteen miles long, has long been connected to the Scottish mainland by a ferry service from Wemyss Bay, making it an attractive holiday location for visitors from Glasgow and the Clyde coast from the mid 19th century.

above: Whelk gatherers sit in their boat at low tide at Kerrycroy, 1903. Postcards on Bute were not exclusively restricted to the conventional and expected tourist images.

It is one of the great delights of Edwardian postcards that they do not just show us the tourist haunts, but give us a complete visual picture of an area. The range of postcards available for visitors to the Isle of Bute included pictures of farms and fishermen as well as the more traditional tourist images of Kerrycroy, Ettrick Bay Port Bannantyne, Mount Stuart and Rothesay.

Holidays on the Isle of Bute, and especially its main town Rothesay, started to grow in popularity from the first half of the 19th century. Steamers were introduced on the route between Wemyss Bay and Rothesay, bringing visitors from Glasgow. By the end of the century, Rothesay itself was one of the most popular destinations for both day trippers and those planning a longer stay.

For as long as Glaswegians went 'doon the watter' they flocked in their tens of thousands to the island, turning Rothesay into the West of Scotland's most popular holiday destination. The contrast between the grime of Glasgow's factories and shipyards and the lush farmlands of Bute and the bright lights of Rothesay could not have been more marked. The one-hour crossing from Wemyss Bay must have seemed like a journey to a different world.

Rothesay took its role as a seaside resort very

Far left: *Horse-drawn omnibuses and their passengers at Kerrycroy, c.1906*

Left: *Rothesay's East Princes Street in 1907.*

main picture: *Photographed by R Whiteford of Rothesay, this view, entitled "Farm Yard Scene (East side of Ettrick Bay)" was published as a postcard before 1904. Images like this perpetuated the 'quaint rural image' of Scotland which had been romanticised since Queen Victoria started to holiday in Balmoral half a century earlier.*

seriously, reclaiming land along the shore to create the flambouyant Victorian Promenade which we still see today. In the early years of the 19th century, the shoreline was some 200 yards further inland!

By the height of its popularity there was also a golf course for the more affluent visitors, opened in 1892.

At the start of the 20th century, the Rothesay Tramway Company (which had operated horse-drawn trams along the front since 1879) invested in an electric tramway service (*opposite*) which opened in 1902. This service actually survived until well into the 1930s.

above: This view of an outdoor tearoom near Kildavanan on Ettrick Bay in 1907 underlines the dress code expected even on holiday. The attire of the holidaymakers must have contrasted vividly with the working clothes of those whose livelihood depended upon the island and its coast.

left: Two women selling their fish on Rothesay Pier, c.1908, while small boys do what small boys do: play on the railings!

main picture: The Promenade and The Car & Brake Terminus, Rothesay, from a postcard mailed in 1907 - 5 years after the introduction of electric trams.

below left: The Royal Navy's Cruiser Squadron (some of Britain's largest fighting ships) moored off Rothesay in 1904.

below right: Rothesay Pier, c.1906, with a cargo vessel moored on the inside of the pier. It was here that the steamers from Wemyss Bay disembarked holidaymakers.

INVERARAY

above: Passengers at Inveraray Pier disembarking from the 1891-built steamer PS Lord of the Isles. *Based on a photograph, taken in the 1890s by Valentines of Dundee, the funnel livery identifies her as belonging to the Glasgow and Inveraray Steamboat Company*

Inveraray was once a successful fishing port when herring was abundant in the loch and Loch Fyne kippers were renowned throughout the land.

At the height of the steamer era, boats ran from Inverary to Glasgow and several piers along the Clyde. A service between Oban, Inveraray and Loigoilhead was established as early as 1827 by the Loch Goil and Loch Long Steamboat Company. The cruise up Loch Fyne was a slow and spectacular way of seeing the finest of Scotland's scenery. Scenes like this are a thing of the past, as today's visitors come by coach and by car. The steamer services ceased in the 1940s.

To cope with the expanding steamer traffic, Inveraray stone pier was extended in the late 19th century and again in the early years of the 20th.

TARBERT, KINTYRE

above: The paddle steamer Columba *is seen here taking on passengers at Tarbert Pier on Loch Fyne, c.1903. This beautiful vessel – often described as the finest paddle steamer ever built – was already 25 years old when this picture was taken. She was built in 1878 specially for David MacBrayne's 'Royal Route to the Isles' and operated for most of her 60 year service life between Glasgow, Tarbert and Ardrishaig. She had undergone a major refit 3 years before this picture was taken, during which she was equipped with lighter and more powerful engines. Their installation brought about such a reduction in weight that thereafter she floated five inches higher in the water! Also added at the time of the refit was a smoking saloon on the promenade deck (the small roofed construction which can be seen just behind the aft funnel). Inside, the ship offered luxury and elegance hitherto unknown on west coast steamers. During the 1900 refit, her saloons were fitted with plush seating, the dining rooms were completely refurbished and MacBrayne's brought in photographers to take a series of photographs of her inside and out. These were used to illustrate the company's 1902 edition of their annual guide book 'Summer Tours in Scotland by David MacBrayne's Royal Mail Steamers Columba, Iona Etc', published in hardback, bound in red linen cloth and priced at one shilling. A quality publication to promote a luxury service!*

left: The fleet setting out to sea from Tarbert, c.1908. Like so many postcards of the period, this was based on a photograph taken about a decade earlier by one of the photographers working for James Valentine of Dundee. At the time, Tarbert had a fishing industry to rival many of the east coast ports. The fishing fleet and the fishwives gutting herring on the quay were popular subjects for photography.*

Isle of Arran

right: *Crouched over the ball, pipe in mouth, a golfer prepares to make his final putt on the golf course at Lamlash, c.1906. In the distance can be seen the hills of Holy Isle. Despite having a par of only 64 today, the golf course has some memorable and demanding holes and has been challenging golfers for well over 100 years.*

below: *Outside the Lamlash Hotel, horses are being readied for their day's work which probably involved taking visitors on sightseeing trips around the area. These carts were also used to take passengers to and from the ferries.*

The isle of Arran was an especially remote place until the introduction of a regular steamer service in the 1820s. The steamship *Helensburgh* started visiting the island in 1827, linking Arran, Cumbrae and Bute and Greenock on the mainland. At that time, with a population in excess of six thousand, the islanders were largely self-sufficient.

It was not until the 1870s that the island got its first proper pier (at Brodick) and piers quickly followed at Lamlash, Lochranza and Whiting Bay, bringing a large increase in the number of tourists visiting the island. By the early years of the 20th century, by which time the Highland Clearances had taken place and a significant number of islanders had emigrated to America and Canada, tourism had become an increasingly important aspect of the island's economy.

Despite Brodick developing as the more popular point of arrival on the island for visitors, Lamlash was a regular port of call for the Royal Navy thanks to the sheltered deep waters of Lamlash Bay. Indeed, the public hall in the village was originally built as a naval canteen. Golfers among the officers of the warships were given complementary membership of the village's challenging little golf course during their stay.

above left: From a series of postcards showing rural aspects of life on Arran, a farmer is busy at work in front of a row of thatched cottages at Sand Braes, Whiting Bay, while several of the locals pose in front of their homes. "This is a lonely place", wrote Mr Macceson to a friend in Bradford in 1904, "could stop here for a month."

above: A steamer leaving Lamlash Pier, c.1905, with Goatfell in the distance. For a time in the Victorian era, Lamlash rivalled Brodick as the main port of entry to Arran. Development of better facilities at Brodick to the north left Lamlash as a quiet picturesque backwater.

left: A puffer makes it way past the fleet at anchor in Lamlash Bay, with Holy Isle in the distance, c.1903.

left: The Bowling Green and Pier, Lamlash, photographed in 1904. A steamer is tied up at the pier and a battleship lies offshore at anchor. Two men get on with the serious business of playing bowls. Royal Navy warships were frequent visitors to the waters around Arran and naval officers were welcome to play at Lamlash Golf Course whenever their ships were in the bay.

CAMPBELTOWN

right: A group of local men and children pose for the camera in front of the 1600 year old Celtic Cross which still stands in the town centre. This view dates from around 1904 and was published by Tucks.

below: A sailing ship at Campbeltown's Old Quay c.1904. The turbine steamer tied up at the end of the quay is believed to be the 554-ton 1901-built King Edward, *the slightly smaller sister ship to the 1902* Queen Alexandra *shown below right.*

below right: A huge crowd awaits the arrival of the Queen Alexandra *at Campbeltown in 1903. Built specifically for the Glasgow to Campbeltown run, she was, at 270 feet long and 665 tons, the pride of the Turbine Steamers Ltd fleet. She had a short service life and, after a serious fire in 1911, was returned to Denny's Dumbarton shipyards for rebuilding before being sold to the Canadian Pacific Railway.*

'Campbeltown Loch', goes the song, 'I wish you were whisky'. Whisky was an important source of the town's prosperity in Victorian and Edwardian times.

In the early years of the 20th century there were over thirty distilleries in and around the town producing over two million gallons of the 'water of life' each year. Now there are only two, however, and only one of them was actually in production at the time of writing.

Whisky has been made in the little Royal Burgh at the foot of the Kintyre peninsula for almost two centuries and, along with whaling, coal mining and the fishing industry, was a reliable source of employment for the locals.

In the 1890s there were often as many as 600 fishing boats in the harbour! The traffic in and out of the port was such that a lifeboat station was established as early as 1861.

The burgh that was originally known as Lochhead was established by James VI and became Campbeltown in 1667, 120 miles from Glasgow by road and 11 miles from the Mull of Kintyre.

Even in the closing years of the 19th century, reaching the town was a lot easier (and not much slower) by steamer than by road. The journey from Glasgow by water was eighty-three miles! The fastest way of getting there today is by plane to the town's local airport.

Campbeltown even had its own narrow-gauge

railway for a time. It was built in 1877 initially to transport coal from the nearby colliery to the harbour, for shipping to ports all over the west coast of Scotland and across the Irish Sea.

To meet the needs of the growing shipping trade, by the second half of the 19th century the town boasted a large safe harbour and three piers. A small-scale shipbuilding industry thrived well into the 20th century.

On August 1st 1906, the railway was upgraded to passenger-carrying capacity. Known as the Campbeltown and Machrihanish Railway by then, it provided an essential link with the tourist steamers such as the *Davaar* (see the entry for Glasgow) and the *Queen Alexandra* (below left) carrying passengers (many of them golfers) the five miles across the peninsula on the aptly named 'Atlantic Express'. For some of its route through Campbeltown to the quay, the railway ran along the town's streets to a terminus outside the Royal Hotel.

above: Campbeltown High Street on a busy day in 1904. Like so many postcards of the time, locals came out of their shops and houses to pose for the camera.

left: : Campbeltown Pier and Harbour, c.1910. The quayside is piled high with barrels – a commodity used both by the fishing industry and the distilleries. At the end of the pier are (on the right) either the Queen Alexandra *or* King Edward *and (on the left) David MacBrayne's famous steamer* Claymore, *the first new steamer to be built for the MacBrayne line and introduced into service in 1881.*

ARDRISHAIG & CRINAN

The Crinan Canal, opened in 1801 between Ardrishaig and Crinan, was designed to reduce the journey time by boat from Glasgow to Scotland's west coast. Popular with the Ardrishaig herring fishermen, the canal saved them the 125-mile journey round the Kintyre peninsula.

With regular steamer services from Glasgow to Ardrishaig and a passenger steamer through the canal, passengers then transferred to a MacBrayne steamer at Crinan for the onward journey to Oban and the Western Isles. David MacBrayne, who described the Glasgow to Oban summer service via Crinan as his 'Royal Route to the Isles', initiated the route in 1866 with a specially commissioned steamer, the *SS Linnet*.

Today the canal is used by pleasure craft and by the occasional preserved West Coast Puffer.

above: Crammed with passengers, MacBrayne's steamer the SS Linnet *(already almost 40 years old) makes its way along the Crinan Canal in 1905. She worked the 8.5 mile route along the canal for 63 years before being sold in 1929. She was destroyed in a storm 3 years later.*

right: The paddle steamer Columba *disembarking passengers at Ardrishaig, c.1904.* Columba *was the largest steamer on the Clyde when she was launched in 1878, and spent nearly 60 years in service. At 600 tons and over 300 feet long, she had been built by J. & G. Thomson of Clydebank especially for the Glasgow to Ardrishaig service.*

above: A solitary crewman stands looking out to sea from the stern of the SS Linnet *tied up at Crinan basin c.1903. A small steam fishing boat, its deck laden with herring barrels, makes its way into the basin through one of the canal locks.*

left: A quiet street scene in Ardrishaig c.1904, bought by a holidaymaker from Sittingbourne in Kent in 1905. Like many visitors, 'Mary' took some of her postcards home with her and used them subsequently to contact friends. As an interesting note on the postal system, Mary's card, posted at 2.30pm to an address in Fareham, has the simple message "If I can manage, I shall be down later this afternoon." The people of Ardrishaig are unlikely ever to have enjoyed a postal service that efficient!

A coach and horses laden with tourists make their way through the Pass of Melfort near Oban in this colourful postcard from the early 1900s. The picture, originally taken in late Victorian times, was used as a postcard subject for many years – sometimes in sepia, black and white and (here) tinted to recreate real colour.

OBAN

For today's travellers, Oban is synonymous with Caledonian MacBrayne and the ferries to the Western Isles. For over a century, it has been the gateway to the islands and the western highlands. A century ago, MacBrayne's ran steamers from Oban to nearly twenty destinations. Today, the network of services from Oban is a far cry from the days when the port was described as the 'Charing Cross of the Highlands'.

David MacBrayne's 1897 handbook advertised routes from Oban to, among other places, Skye (with a choice of arriving at Portree, Broadford, Armadale, Isle Ornsay, Dunvegan or Kyleakin), Islay, Iona, Staffa, Mull, Coll, Tiree, Lochboisdale Tarbert Loch Fyne and Tarbert Harris, Ardrishaig, Gairloch, Ullapool, Stornoway and even Inverness.

Oban was developed in Victorian times from a small fishing village into the most important town on this stretch of the west coast, boasting several top quality hotels as well as its thriving port.

The colosseum-like structure which dominates the Oban skyline was a 'job-creation scheme' well before such things became fashionable.

Local businessman and banker John McCaig funded the construction in the late 1890s to alleviate unemployment, at a personal cost of over £5000. Work started in 1897 but McCaig died before even the shell was finished; the construction was never completed.

As he apparently envisaged a museum with statues of his ancestors looking out over the town, few regretted the fact that his grandiose plans never came to fruition!

top: Pleasure craft at anchor in Oban Bay, c.1903

below: Oban from the New Pier – showing the Station Hotel, McCaig's Tower and the elegant Esplanade, from a 1906 postcard.

59

MALLAIG

above: A long West Highland Express train, pulled by two North British Railway locomotives, makes its way along the single track line towards Mallaig in 1908, 7 years after the West Highland Railway's Mallaig Extension Railway line had been opened. By that time it had already been swallowed up by the much larger North British Railway, of which it had actually been a subsidiary company since the line as far as Fort William was first proposed in 1889.

Mallaig is one of a number of British ports which have laid claim to the distinction of once being the busiest herring port in Europe! This is quite a claim for a town which didn't exist until just over a century ago, and which actually came into being by accident.

One hundred and fifty miles north of Glasgow, with sparse transport links throughout the 19th century (very poor roads and no railway), Mallaig may seem an unusual location for such a successful port especially as the town's fishermen did not have a centuries-old tradition behind them.

The fishing fleet arrived only after a railway link (the Mallaig Extension Railway) had been established in 1901. Judging by the length of the train in the above photograph, by 1908 the line was proving immensely popular to fishermen and travellers alike.

Before then, Mallaig was just a tiny village. The

railway only adopted Mallaig as its terminus because the rights to build the track along its originally intended route could not be acquired at an economic price. From those accidental beginnings Mallaig grew into a major fishing port, employing hundreds of people on the boats and on the quayside.

With the railway came a pier, regular train services to Fort William, Inverness and central Scotland and ferry links to Skye, opening the new port up to a growing Edwardian tourist trade.

David MacBrayne, whose steamer company was already 50 years old in 1901, established the first ferry service from the new pier in that year and (as CalMac) that service continues to this day.

However, as few people spent any time in the town Victorian and Edwardian photographers largely passed it by. Few postcards of Mallaig were produced in the early years of last century; of those which were, they rarely did the town any favours!

ULLAPOOL

Unlike Mallaig, Ullapool's history as a fishing port goes back to the 18th century when the waters of Loch Broom were regularly teeming with herring. Plans to establish a fishing station were actually first discussed in the late 17th century, but it was almost a century before those plans were translated into the development of the village and harbour at Ullapool.

It was in 1788 that the British Fisheries Society actually established their fishing station on the shore of Loch Broom, and employed Thomas Telford to design the little town. Much of what can be seen today still bears Telford's hallmark.

By the 1830s, intensive fishing had virtually stripped the loch of its herring and the fishermen were (not for the last time) facing ruin.

The herring stocks recovered to an extent,

and fishing and fish processing continued to be a significant local employer throughout the 19th century and into the 20th. Salted and pickled herring is exported from Ullapool to Ireland, Sweden and elsewhere.

However, the port's limited transport link remained a major barrier to real expansion. Ullapool's hopes of being linked to the rest of the country by railway, although approved by parliament, were never realised. It was not until long after the period embraced by this book that Ullapool enjoyed real commercial success.

It was not as a herring port that this revival came about, however, but thanks to the growing world popularity of the humble mackerel the safe waters of Loch Broom have became the seasonal base for fishing fleets from around the world.

below: Ullapool's fishing boats setting sail out of Loch Broom – an evocative view from around 1900. By the time this picture was taken, the herring were in decline and the town appeared to be facing commercial ruin. More than a century later, the port still supports a small fishing fleet.

ISLE OF SKYE

below: This image, entitled 'Herring Fishing at Portree', was published by local stationer J W Dickson before 1906. It shows fishermen preparing their herring smacks for another day's fishing. At the top of the slip, a small group of fisher girls, surrounded by barrels, are gutting and packing the catch.

Until the arrival of the railway at Kyle of Lochalsh in 1897, most visitors to Skye came by steamer to the island's capital Portree. It was described in John Bartholomew's 1887 *Gazetteer of the British Isles* as "pop. 893; situated on a commodious land-locked harbour, and is regularly visited by Glasgow steamers".

Victorian Skye changed dramatically between the 1840s and the 1880s. An estimated 30,000 people left the island during those decades, as crofters were ousted from their land by profiteering landowners who saw greater returns from sheep grazing than from the meagre rents they could charge the crofters.

The riots which followed in 1882 (known locally as the Battle of the Braes) set the crofters against several dozen Glasgow policemen who had been shipped over to the island to maintain order. The police were eventually reinforced by marines landed from naval vessels at Uig pier.

Public abhorrence at the plight of the crofters and the excessive force used to quell them eventually led to the Crofters' Act. Passed in 1886, it gave them much-needed security of tenancy.

above: Climbers on the 'Inaccessible Pinnacle', Isle of Skye, photographed by the legendary mountaineering photographers Abrahams of Keswick, c.1905. This dramatic view was No. 50 in their popular series of rock climbing postcards. While Bute and Arran were magnets for tourists, the rugged and mountainous landscape of Skye attracted climbers from all over the country.

The popularity of rock climbing dates only from the middle of the 19th century and, until 1856, the many mountain peaks on Skye had never been climbed. Over the following 20 years, most of them were conquered by climbers from Glasgow. From the 1880s, with a railway terminus only ten miles from Skye, climbers from much further a-field found travel to the island faster and easier and came in large numbers to tackle its peaks and cliffs. It is reckoned that by the end of Victoria's reign, every peak and pinnacle on the island had been climbed, as had most of the dramatic rock faces.

top: Looking over the rooftops of Kyle of Lochalsh, towards Kyleakin, c.1902. The railway had opened only 5 years earlier, bringing with it considerable growth in commercial shipping and, of course, the short ferry crossing to Skye. Before 1902, most travellers arrived on Skye by steamer from Glasgow and Oban, sailing directly to Kyleakin, Armadale, Isle Ornsay, Dunvegan or Totaig, Portree and Broadford.

above: Skye Crofters cottages on the shore, photographed by or for James Valentine and Sons c.1904. These traditional cottages are known as 'black houses' in the islands. Despite their thick stone walls and thatched or turfed roofs, they cannot have offered much comfort in the extremes of Skye weather.

LEWIS & HARRIS

above: Bringing home the peats, from a photograph c.1900. This back-breaking work was undertaken by the women.

above right: A Lewis crofting family pose for the camera outside their house in 1902.

opposite page: Herring barrels line the quayside at Stornoway, the island's capital and centre of the fishing industry.

The islanders of Lewis and Harris (parts of the same island) have long been dependent on fishing, crofting and weaving for their livelihood and on their abundant supply of peat for their fuel. The surviving images of the islands from Victorian and Edwardian times reflect the harshness of the islanders' existence, often romanticising it for a more sophisticated postcard-buying public.

Hundreds of thousands of barrels of preserved and pickled fish were exported through Stornoway harbour every year at the height of the herring fishing industry in the early 20th century, providing a great deal of local employment.

So important was the fishing industry, that when a new Fish Mart was planned in the 1890s the trading floor was designed to accommodate 250 traders! It was to be built at a cost of £1200 and sited so it did not obstruct the view from the castle across the harbour.

Undoubtedly the most famous commodity to come from the islands is Harris Tweed, still made today by handloom weavers in their cottages. The weaving of Harris Tweed has always been a cottage industry, although the tweed itself has changed over the years from a robust and hard-wearing fabric to one produced today very much with the fashion industry in mind.

Harris Tweed's popularity started to grow towards the end of the 19th century and, with the passing of the Trade Marks Act in 1905, the islanders sought to strengthen their brand by developing their own trade mark and forming an umbrella organisation to control quality, manufacture and marketing. The Harris Tweed Association was formed in Stornoway in 1909, and their famous 'orb' trademark still graces genuine Harris Tweed today. This is a very early example of the application of a brand identity and manufacturing quality standards, to what was effectively a product produced by independent self-employed workers.

ORKNEY ISLANDS

The town of Stromness, on the south-western tip of Mainland to the west of Scapa Flow, is still a maze of narrow winding streets today. Despite its small size, it was Stromness with its safe sheltered harbour (rather than the Orkneys' capital Kirkwall) which established trading links with North America.

Until 100 years ago, the ships of the Hudson Bay Company regularly took on provisions and water at Stromness and also employed large numbers of local men as crew. Its popularity as a stopover both for transatlantic vessels and for fishing trawlers meant that the resident population was often outnumbered several-fold by visiting sailors and fishermen.

This may explain its unusually large number of inns and taverns. Records show that there were more than three dozen public houses by the middle of the 19th century, in a town with a population of little more than a thousand souls! At times the small village must have exhibited an almost cosmopolitan character.

From around 1880 until the First World War, Stromness was also a busy herring port. Records tell of over 400 boats berthing in and around the harbour at the height of the fishing season. It was, after all, an ideal opportunity for steam trawlers to top up their supplies of coal.

Fishing is still an important employer, but not on such a grand scale.

top: Entitled 'Farewell to Orkney', this unusual photograph depicts cattle being hoisted in cradles into the forward hold of the steamer bound for the Scottish mainland, while passengers look on. As recently as the early 1970s, cars still were loaded on board the Scrabster to Stromness ferry in exactly the same way. The photograph was taken in Stromness and the ship is the North of Scotland, Orkney and Shetland Shipping Company's ferry (702 grt) St Ninian which served the route from 1895 until 1948. Crossing the Pentland Firth in the St Ninian – which had a tendency to roll alarmingly in heavy seas – cannot have been a pleasant experience. She also occasionally sailed out of Wick's Pulteneytown harbour. A regular steamer crossing between Scrabster on the Scottish mainland and Stromness was introduced as early as 1855 and continues to this day.

bottom: Kirkwall Harbour, photographed in the closing years of the 19th century. This view was still available on a postcard well into the first decade of the 20th century. The sailing vessel in the foreground was the Report. Today's Aberdeen to Kirkwall ferry service uses a new linkspan at Hatston Terminal further round the bay, to the north west of the old harbour.

SHETLAND ISLANDS

right: Commercial Street In Lerwick, photographed, c.1905.

below: A Busy scene in Lerwick Harbour around 1908

opposite page top: Whaling employed significant numbers of men on many of the Scottish islands. Christian Salveson established the Olna Whaling Station (photographed by R Ramsay in 1904) on the west coast of the Shetland mainland in 1903.

opposite page bottom: The herring industry was a major local employer with hundreds of local women employed as packers, some of whom posed for this 1904 photograph.

The most northerly of the Scottish islands, the Shetland Isles have a long tradition of living off the sea. Their position on the edge of the European continental shelf with deep waters immediately beyond their shores meant that both fishing and whaling offered rich pickings within relatively short sailing distances. In addition, the kelp harvests around the shores were used in the iodine industry.

Herring fishing on an industrial scale dates only from the second half of the 19th century, and the whaling stations only from the earliest years of the 20th century. Before that, the islands' inshore fishermen went to sea in nothing more than large rowing boats: a perilous occupation indeed!

The industry grew in importance rapidly throughout the 1880s and 1890s, and peaked in 1905 when over a million barrels of herring were exported from the islands.

This expansion came about at a time when crofters were being driven off the land to make way for sheep, either emigrating or making their way to the coastal towns and villages for work. At the end of the century the Shetlands had a population of almost 32,000.

below: Despite the appearance of broad daylight, this unusual picture of Lerwick Town Hall was photographed under the midnight sun on June 29th 1889 and subsequently tinted and published in 1905.

WICK & PULTENEYTOWN

The Royal Burgh of Wick can trace its origins back to the late 16th century and, despite its later 19th century fame, for most of the intervening years it was described as a small and poor burgh. Fishing had been a mainstay of local employment probably at least since the Vikings, but not on the scale necessary to bring significant wealth to the area.

Change came in the early years of the 19th century with the development of the new town and harbour at Pulteneytown, named after a local visionary Sir William Pulteney who saw a great future in fishing.

Thomas Telford designed the new harbour, and by the middle of the century Pulteney Harbour was renowned as not just the largest herring port in Scotland, but in the whole of Europe.

Over one thousand craft used the harbour in the 1860s and 1870s, and Pulteneytown on the south bank of the River Wick became important enough to be administratively independent of Wick on the north bank until 1902.

A fleet of that size employed a considerable number of people, but they represented only a small fraction of the number whose livelihood depended on the fishing industry. Hundreds were employed in gutting and pickling the fish, and many more were employed as coopers, carriers and crews for the ships which dispersed the catch around Scotland and across to the west coast of Europe: around 8000 in total

Many of those workers and their families went to the Jonhston studio to have their portraits taken. Alexander Johnston encouraged them to pose with the tools of their trades, creating a priceless pictorial legacy of the glory days. Because the Johnstons never threw anything away their collection of glass negatives still survives, preserved for future generations by the Wick Society.

By 1900 the fishing industry was showing signs of decline and, by the 1930s, the number of fishing boats working out of the harbour had reduced to fewer than thirty. Today oil plays a more important part in the local economy than fishing.

INVERGORDON

Known as Inverbreakie until redeveloped by Sir William Gordon in the 18th century, Invergordon became an important port and military base during Queen Victoria's reign. Royal navy ships used the anchorage for much of the 19th century, but it was only at the dawn of the 20th century that an official naval base was established. Drawn by the safe deep anchorage the Cromarty Firth offered, a dockyard and facilities for fuelling both coal-fired and oil-fired steamers were provided.

By 1907, visits from the Home Fleet were becoming commonplace. In that year, one such visit saw a dozen battleships, six cruisers, over twenty other vessels and over fourteen thousand men visit the port.

The navy left in the 1950s, and thereafter the town reinvented itself as a key player in the North Sea oil business.

Today the former Admiralty Pier annually plays host to up to four dozen visiting cruise ships.

above: A sailing ship lies at Invergordon quay c.1905. The harbour was extended in the early 19th century, and the port went on to become an important naval base and 'the finest deep water anchorage in Europe'.

left: Local publishers, the MacPherson Brothers (with premises in Invergordon, Tain and Beauly) published this remarkable postcard of the huge storms which lashed the Cromarty Firth and Invergordon's sea wall on June 16th 1904. It was taken from near the Ship Inn on the seafront; the chimney to the right of the picture belongs to a large sawmill sited next to the railway station.

INVERNESS
& THE CALEDONIAN CANAL

right: Dundee photographers and publishers James Valentine & Son first marketed this delightful postcard in black and white in 1902 or 1903. This tinted example followed a couple of years later. Entitled 'Inverness from Friar's Shott', it is more a study of the children than it is of the city itself. Despite its importance, Inverness does not seem to have been blessed with many interesting postcards during this period. This placid scene on the River Ness is in sharp contrast to that which would be seen after heavy rains and high tides. In winter the fast-flowing river was – and still is – prone to flooding. Over the centuries it has swept away several of the bridges spanning it, including a fine 250-year old seven-arch stone bridge which collapsed in 1849.

Despite having a relatively small population (under 20,000) and poor transport links, Inverness was a thriving industrial and commercial centre in the second half of the 19th century. Local trades included wooden shipbuilding and the associated trades of sail and rope making, as well as agriculture, whisky distilling, brewing and a wide range of merchants and ships' chandlers handling the goods which passed through the city's quays.

The importance of the town was increased with the opening of the Caledonian Canal in 1822, but the first railway link was not established until 1854 (and that was only from Nairn, a few miles to the northeast). A north–south link via Aviemore did not open until 1898.

The city was an important staging post for people as well as goods, including the many military personnel who garrisoned places such as Fort George along the Moray Firth, so it is perhaps surprising that the railway arrived so late.

Despite the fact that the Caledonian Canal (Thomas Telford's engineering masterpiece) was not a financial success, it gave Inverness vital transport links with the south.

David MacBrayne's 1897 timetable records that their 281 ton paddle steamer *Fusilier* regularly travelled the length of the canal, carrying passengers to and from Inverness, Fort Augustus, Ballachulish and Oban. 'Swift Steamers' were the fastest and for 22 shillings per single ticket, travellers to Oban could enjoy the luxury of the steamer's cabin. Over half that amount could be saved by travelling 'steerage' on deck for 10s.6d. Return tickets cost 33 and 16 shillings respectively – a considerable saving. The steamer left Oban at 6.00 am each day, arriving at Inverness at 5.30 pm.

For those with time to spare, a service from Glasgow to Inverness (via Crinan and Oban) on the paddle steamer Cavalier left the Clyde at 1 pm on Mondays, arriving at the quayside in Inverness at 4 pm each Wednesday. For the passengers who could afford the trip, their overnight cabins were advertised as having the luxury of electric lights!

above: Steamers sailed regularly to Inverness via the Caledonian Canal from several ports and jetties on the west coast. At the southern end, having first called in at Corpach Pier at the top of Loch Linnhe, the boats entered the canal at Fort William through a single sea lock before entering the flight of eight locks at Banavie known as Neptune's Staircase. This view of MacBrayne's paddle steamer Fusilier dates from around 1908. On the pier, a horse-drawn omnibus stands by having just disembarked its passengers.

left: At the northern end of the canal just south of Inverness, four boats (fishing boats judging by their registration) are just leaving the lock at Tomnahurich. West coast fishermen regularly used the canal, especially during the herring season, as a means of getting to the rich fishing grounds in the North Sea. The canal, still a favoured 'short cut' for trawlers today, meets the Beauly Firth at Clachnaharry.

75

FRASERBURGH

below: "There's nothing but herring here" wrote Annie to Mrs Allan of Peterculter on the back of this postcard in August 1903! This scene was photographed and published by George Washington Wilson of Aberdeen, and probably dates from the late 1890s. The studio had dominated the market for Scottish scenic views since the 1860s, and moved into postcard production in 1902.

Estimates of the size of Fraserburgh's herring fleet in the late 19th century range from just under 700 to over 1000 boats. Certainly, there are said to have been about 700 registered in the port. Many others also used the port; for example, the boat in the foreground of the photograph, below, was registered to J. M. Wallace from Nairn.

That puts the fleet larger than either Stornoway or Aberdeen, about the same size as Pulteneytown at Wick.

It was claimed that the harbour, like Pulteneytown, could handle up to one thousand herring smacks at a time.

The annual herring catch made Fraserburgh into a thriving town, employed a significant proportion of the local workforce and also provided work right down the east coast for the 'Scotch Fish Girls'. Like their counterparts at Peterhead, see opposite, they travelled with the herring shoals as they moved south through the season. There is still a fishing fleet at the port today, and Fraserburgh's fish markets remain among the busiest in Scotland.

PETERHEAD

Peterhead has long depended on the sea for its livelihood. At the beginning of the Victorian era, it was one of the largest and most important whaling ports in Britain.

Whaling had disappeared by the end of the century, however. The last whaling ship to dock at Peterhead did so in 1893. In addition, it supported a fishing fleet which grew in size as the 19th century progressed. From fewer than two dozen boats in 1830, the fleet had increased to 250 within a decade and to more than 400 by 1850!

With a fine harbour, Peterhead was ideally placed to capitalise on the growing demand for herring throughout the Victorian period. By the end of the century, it rivalled Aberdeen in terms of the size and importance of its fleet.

The herring season was short (from mid July to the end of September). During that period, however, over five thousand itinerant workers arrived in the town to work on the fish quays, in the fish curing facilities and in packing and transporting the fish. As the herring stocks dwindled, Peterhead fishermen went further a-field in search of white fish.

As well as those directly employed in the catching, processing and packing of the fish, the trade supported nearly 500 coopers making the barrels into which the herring were packed. The arrival of a ship carrying cheaper foreign-made barrels in 1893 provoked a riot, as the coopers saw their livelihood threatened. That was the beginning of the end, as although they refused to allow the completed barrels to be unloaded, they could not stop tons of ready-shaped staves being landed and used.

above: Peterhead's fishing fleet setting sail c.1903, from a Reliable Series 'Chromotype' postcard printed in Hessen, Germany. The fleet was still predominantly sail, although one steam trawler can be seen leading the ships out to sea in this photograph.

right: Peterhead's fish girls gutted and packed herring not only in their home port. As the herring moved south down through the North Sea the girls also travelled south, working at fishing ports as far a-field as Great Yarmouth in Norfolk. Specially organised trains took them to Scarborough, Whitby, Grimsby and many other herring ports along the east coast. 'Scotch Fish Girls' featured in photographs and postcards published throughout the later Victorian era and the Edwardian years. This was hard and often painful work. They frequently cut themselves while gutting up to 60 fish a minute, and then had to work with the salt used to preserve the fish in barrels!

ABERDEEN

Aberdeen was an important centre of ship-building for centuries. Aberdeen-built tea clippers (such as the *Thermopylae*) were as renowned in their day as the *Cutty Sark*, built on the more famous Clyde.

Aberdeen was, for centuries, one of the most important fishing ports on Scotland's east cost, with over 700 sailing trawlers operating out of the port in the last quarter of the 19th century

With the advent of steam power, the Aberdeen trawler fleet regenerated the city's fortunes. Steam power also increased the city's importance as a whaling port. Today and for the past three decades, however, it has been known the world over as Scotland's oil capital.

Where once there were hundreds of fishing boats, today there is all the paraphernalia necessary to serve one of the most challenging of today's energy industries. Where once huge fishmarkets lined the quays and where fisherwomen gutted and pickled herring can now be found all the specialist services required by the multi-million pound offshore oil extraction companies.

Victorian photographers such as George Washington Wilson (an Aberdeen man whose catalogue of images covered the whole country by the 1870s) and the photographers who later served the Edwardian postcard makers all preserved these exciting years in the city's development. Victorian and Edwardian Aberdeen was both an industrial centre and a popular tourist destination, and was very proud of its beautiful beaches.

More than any other of Scotland's major Victorian and Edwardian east coast ports, Aberdeen's transformation has been enormous.

above left: Fishwives on Aberdeen's quayside pose for the camera c.1904.

left: Promenading above the long stretches of beautiful beach, Edwardian Aberdonians seem a million miles away from the bustle of the fish quays. Bathing machines and all the other trappings of the seaside holiday were available on their doorstep.

opposite page: This remarkable view of Aberdeen harbour comes from a 1904 picture postcard, published by Valentine of Dundee. While steam ships predominate, there are still a considerable number of sailing vessels using the harbour.

above and right: Many of Aberdeen's Edwardian postcards captured the bustle of the fish quays and fish markets, and almost boasted about the enormous catches which were landed every day of the week.

below: Another of the city's many postcards celebrating its success as a holiday resort contrasts vividly with the industrial scenes above and to the right.

top: Postcards showing the bustle of the fish quays and fish markets were just as popular with locals (who used them regularly to communicate with each other) as they were with visitors. This 1905 view shows the busy quayside with part of the day's catch already landed.

above: A busy day in Aberdeen Docks photographed in 1902. While steamers line the near quay, the vessels on the opposite side are all sailing ships.

right: Busy quaysides, Aberdeen Harbour 1904, with a mixture of sailing vessels and small steam ships.

STONEHAVEN

above left: The fishing quarter, Stonehaven, from a postcard mailed to an address in Folkestone in 1908.

above right: Shelling Mussels, Old Town, Stonehaven, from a Valentine postcard which remained on sale in the town from around 1908 through into the mid 1920s!

above: A summer scene on the beach at Stonehaven c.1906.

By the time the photographs of fisherwomen in the two postcards on this page were taken, the glory days of Stonehaven as a fishing port were effectively over. For much of the 19th century, since the building of the first pier to protect the harbour in 1825, the town had grown steadily as the fishing industry had developed. However, by the time of the completion of the main breakwater in 1908, fewer than 20 fishing boats were based in the harbour. Thirty years earlier there had been 80.

Never a major port on the scale of Aberdeen or Peterhead, Stonehaven's fishing industry had, nonetheless, been a major employer.

Stonehaven was designated the county town of Kincardineshire in 1600, but saw little expansion until the second half of the 18th century when the new town was laid out. The 19th century development of the harbour was engineered by Robert Stevenson.

Stonehaven was also the home of Robert William Thomson who, in 1845, invented the pneumatic tyre, some 40 years before the name of John Dunlop entered the history books.

above and left: Two animated views of Stonehaven harbour, both dating from 1903.

Montrose

In 1887, John Bartholomew's *Gazetteer of the British Isles* noted that "The harbour, comprising the reach of the river from the suspension bridge to the sea, is naturally deep and well sheltered, and the quays are well constructed and commodious. The trade with the Baltic and Canada is considerable."

One of the more elegant of the east coast holiday resorts, Montrose has a long and rich history. Throughout the Victorian and Edwardian period, Montrose enjoyed well-established trading links with many ports in the Baltic and northern Europe.

In Victorian times, the town was renowned not just as a fishing and shipping centre and as a holiday resort (thanks to its harbour and extensive sands) but also as one of the country's leading centres of golf. The game was first played here in the mid 17th century and, in the 1860s, the town boasted a lengthy 25-hole course!

The town's links course is still rated as one of the finest in the country, and was used as one of the final qualifying courses for the Open Championship in both 1999 and 2007.

opposite page: Montrose beach, c.1902, with candy-striped bathing machines

above: FFishermen beaching their boats near Scurdie Ness Lighthouse at Montrose Point, 1902. The 39 m tall lighthouse (also known as Scurdyness) was opened in 1870 to warn mariners of this treacherous stretch of rocky coastline.

left: Traders selling their wares on Montrose's 18th century High Street (renowned as the widest High Street in Scotland) c.1905.

ARBROATH

right: Storm waves lashing Arbroath quay featured on several Edwardian postcards. This was photographed in 1908.

far right: Arbroath harbour, from a 1905 view, with a three-masted sailing vessel preparing for departure and a small steamer tied up further down the quay.

below: Men and women packing herring on Arbroath quay: a scene typical of many east coast ports in Edwardian times. The packers were predominantly women, while most of the men were involved in making and sealing the barrels. Judging by the number of wooden straps visible in the bottom right of this picture, barrel-making was undertaken on a quite significant scale. Each barrel held an average of around one thousand fish.

Arbroath's place in Scotland's turbulent history needs no further explanation here. The ruins of the abbey brought many of the early photographers and postcard publishers to the town.

From an employment point of view, however, it was the harbour which was the focus of 19th century attention.

Although a harbour had existed in the town since mediaeval times, it was extensively rebuilt and expanded in the late 18th century, enabling it to attract considerable Baltic trade.

The fishing fleet, which had been long established both at Arbroath and nearby Auchmithie (the original home of the Arbroath Smokie) grew considerably as ship owners moved from other ports, attracted by the improved facilities.

Arbroath was not just a one-fish port; large quantities of both herring and haddock as well as lobster and crab were landed on its quays throughout the Victorian and Edwardian eras until the 20th century. At its peak, there were about 150 boats registered in the town, many of them bringing in catches of haddock. Salted and smoked over an oak fire, the haddock were transformed into the legendary Arbroath Smokie which is still produced in the town today.

The arrival of the Dundee and Arbroath Railway in 1839 (fully opened in 1840) did much to boost the fortunes of existing industries by offering quicker delivery of materials and distribution of manufactured goods. Before the arrival of the railway, most of the town's needs were brought in by coastal steamer.

Arbroath had a long tradition of weaving and a thriving sailcloth industry. By the 1870s, there were more than thirty textile mills in the town producing half a million yards of cloth each year and employing many local people. This was, sadly, rather fewer than had worked the handlooms of the 18th century.

CARNOUSTIE

Carnoustie is one of those Scottish towns whose name is synonymous with golf. It has long been recognised as having one of the country's finest links courses, and is still one of the venues for the Open (most recently hosted in 2007).

The town owes its existence to sandy beaches and fine golf courses, of which it now has three; hence its profusion of hotels and guesthouses .

Records suggest that golf has been played on the town's links since at least the beginning of the 16th century, and probably earlier. Despite its long-standing golfing tradition, it was not until 1931 that Carnoustie first hosted the Open. By that time, Allan Robertson's 1842 ten-hole course had been extended to eighteen holes by 'Old' Tom Morris in 1867. It has been extensively remodelled on at least two further occasions. Carnoustie is proud of having established the country's first ladies' golf club. This was founded in 1873 at a time when golf was a jealously guarded male preserve.

above: Golf on Carnoustie Links, c.1904. The course was originally designed by the great 'Old' Tom Morris in the 1860s. It was only the second eighteen-hole course to be opened in Scotland, although a ten-hole course had existed here since the 1830s. This card was posted from Barry Camp, a huge army camp just outside the town. Military officers often boasted in the 1890s that their posting allowed them to play golf most afternoons!

left: Carnoustie Promenade c.1905. The town's position just a few miles from Dundee made it an ideal holiday location.

overleaf: Carnoustie High Street c.1906

BROUGHTY FERRY

left: A nanny pushes her charge along the seafront in Broughty Ferry, c.1908, while a crowd of holidaymakers watches a performance by the Bachelor Boys on the small stage set up on the beach. The Bachelor Boys were regular summer visitors to the resort, performing there for several years before the Great War.

below: North Gray Street, Broughty Ferry, photographed in 1906. The level-crossing gates have just been closed to await the arrival of a train on the railway line from Dundee to Carnoustie. Some of the large houses up the hill were owned by those who controlled the jute trade in nearby Dundee.

As the name suggests, Broughty Ferry was once the landing point for the Tay ferry, but those days had long ceased by the time the pictures here were taken. A small harbour once played host to a few fishing boats, but they too had gone by the end of Victoria's reign.

From the middle of the 19th century the town started to develop as a holiday resort. With good railway access and fines beaches, it attracted holidaymakers from throughout eastern Scotland, and was also only a short travelling distance from Dundee for those seeking a day at the seaside.

With Dundee only three miles away, many of the jute magnates who had made or were making their fortunes in the city built elegant villas on the hill overlooking the old village towards the end of the century. They had the double benefit of being close to work and living in a rural environment. It was said that Broughty Ferry was, as a result of their patronage, richer than any other town of comparable size in Scotland.

DUNDEE

Dundee's history is a long and distinguished one. Despite a seafaring tradition which goes back to mediaeval times (certainly as far back as the 13th century), its history as one of the major seaports on Scotland's east coast dates back only as far as 1825 when the King William IV Dock was opened.

Between then and the 1860s, the population almost trebled to over ninety thousand. By the end of the 19th century, almost 30,000 people were employed in the textile industry alone.

The history of early 19th century employment in the town was dominated by textiles: first flax and then jute. By the 1820s there were seventeen flax-weaving mills included in the total of nearly fifty textile companies. The introduction of power looms and jute weaving, pioneered in the town in the early 1820s, was responsible for a further significant growth. By the 1860s, there were over fifty large weaving mills and the docks were handling over 40,000 tons of jute imports annually. By the mid 1870s, that had almost quadrupled. By the 1990s, however, only one jute weaver from a very few surviving textile manufacturers remained in the city.

Queen Victoria visited Dundee in 1844. To commemorate her visit, the Norman-style Royal Arch was completed 4 years later at what was then the substantial cost of £2270. The city was in the ascendancy at the time, and that first visit from a reigning monarch since the late 17th century was deemed momentous enough to warrant such an expense.

Earl Grey Dock was completed in 1843, the year before the Queen's visit. By the mid 1860s, it was joined by the Camperdown and Victoria Docks. Whaling was by that time another major industry, as was shipbuilding.

above: The paddle steamer Dundee *leaving Dundee for Newport in 1902. Ferries to Newport ran from 1713 until the opening of the Tay Road Bridge in 1966. The two other ferries which worked the crossing –* Fifeshire *and* Forfarshire *– can be seen to her left.*

left: Murraygate, Dundee, c.1910. A single motor vehicle is driving up the centre of the street while all the other vehicles are horse-drawn.

Both the King William IV and Earl Grey Docks were filled in the 1960s to make way for the infrastructure of the Tay Road Bridge, but the Camperdown Dock today is home to the *Discovery*, Robert Falcon Scott's famous ship. *Discovery* was built in Dundee, to a whaling ship design, and set sail for Antarctica on July 1st 1901. Also moored in Camperdown Dock is the 1824 Chatham-built wooden frigate *HMS Unicorn*. Another casualty of the Tay Road Bridge development, the Royal Arch (which had stood at the entrance to the docks for almost 120 years) was demolished in 1964.

By the 1870s, nearly 300 ships were registered to the port. For 20 years before that, the city had been exporting textile machinery to India. This was a trade which would prove to have long-term and disastrous consequences, the impact of which is still felt today. From the mid 1850s, Dundee mill-owners had also operated mills in India. Within 25 years of that first sale, Indian mills were producing huge quantities of textiles and undercutting the Dundee-made product.

The railway came to the city in three stages. The Dundee and Arbroath Railway linked Dundee with Arbroath to the north from 1839 (with a 5 foot 6 inches gauge) and had its own railway police force from the outset.

The Dundee and Perth Railway opened in 1845, followed by the Edinburgh Perth and Dundee 3 years later, originally using the Forth and Tay ferries. With the opening of the Tay Bridge by the North British Railway in 1878, the city had a direct rail link with Fife and Edinburgh.

above: Dundee Docks and the Royal Arch (erected in 1848 to commemorate a visit from Queen Victoria in 1844) from a photograph taken in the 1890s for the local James Valentine studio, and published as a postcard c.1904. A number of steamships are in evidence, but the profusion of rigging suggests sail was still the most predominant power source.

left: One of James Valentine's early 1880 photographs of the partially collapsed Tay Bridge. Thomas Bouch's bridge had collapsed on 29th December 1879, only 19 months after it had been opened. A southbound train, carrying a 3-man crew and between 60 and 75 passengers, was plunged into the raging river below.

far left: Dundee Docks, c.1908, with the Royal Arch in the background. The King William IV Dock, Dundee's first dock, was opened in 1825.

93

NEWPORT ON TAY & WORMIT

above: The paddle steamer ferry Dundee *disembarking at the Newport slipway, 1903. Built 1875, she served the Tay crossing until 1917 before serving as a cruise ship on the river. A few years later she was back in service as a ferry, this time on the River Forth. She was eventually scrapped in 1952 after 77 years of service.*

Originally known as Seamills or Sea Myles, and later for a short period New Dundee, Newport became the northern embarkation point for the Tay ferry crossing in 1713 and adopted its present name later in the century.

Thomas Telford designed the ferry pier in 1823 just 3 years after steam ferries were introduced on to the route in 1820. The ferry *Union* served the crossing until 1836.

The enhanced ferry service, and the building of the Tay Railway Bridge which opened in 1878, had a major impact on the village. It expanded considerably as wealthy merchants from Dundee chose to move their families across the river to the cleaner air and more rural environment of Newport. With excellent rail and ferry links, the jute capital of Scotland was just a few minutes away. Public confidence in the rail crossing suffered a setback when the first Tay Bridge collapsed in 1879, but recovered with the opening of the new bridge in 1887. After the Tay Road Bridge opened in the 1970s, both ferry and rail links ceased to operate.

left: The Ferry Pier, Newport-on-Tay. The vessel tied up at the slipway is the Clyde-built paddle steamer Fifeshire, built by R. Napier and Sons and brought into service in 1858. She was already over 40 years old when this 1904 photograph was taken. She was one of three vessels working the crossing between Newport and Dundee. Her sister ferry Dundee (built in Renfrew 1875) can be seen opposite. The Fifeshire was replaced by a steel-hulled paddle steamer Newport (the second vessel to bear that name), built by Caledon's in Dundee in 1910. Paddle steamers continued on the service well into the 1950s, with the Sir William High and the B L Nairn (introduced in 1924 and 1929, respectively), albeit working alongside two much more manoeuverable vessels.

left: An eight-carriage train prepares to depart from the curved platform at Wormit Station c.1904 and make its way over the rebuilt Tay Bridge to Dundee. Compared with the original bridge (see previous pages) the replacement bridge was built on much more substantial piers, better able to withstand the storms and high winds for which the Tay estuary is known. The piers of the original bridge have stood out of the water now for a century and a quarter – a constant reminder of the fate which befell the train and its passengers. No-one really knew how many people died. The police gave the death toll as 60, but the railway company believed 75 tickets to Dundee had been sold to passengers boarding the train as it travelled through Fife. With the train crew of 3, that would make 78. Only 60 bodies were ever recovered.

ST ANDREWS

above: St Andrews Harbour from the pier. The harbour was built at the mouth of the Kinness Burn, probably in the 14th century, and by the 15th century enjoyed considerable European trade. St Rule's Tower in the centre of the skyline was already almost 900 years old when this photograph was taken c.1902.

St Andrews, Scotland's oldest seat of learning and the undisputed home of golf, is dominated by the ruins of the great Augustinian Cathedral Priory.

At the height of the city's importance as an ecclesiastical centre, it traded with ports along the west coast of Europe. However, as the importance of St Andrews was steadily eclipsed by the rise of both Edinburgh and Glasgow, the little harbour could not compete.

When this view of the harbour from the end of the pier was taken c.1902 the little city still had a small but thriving inshore fishing fleet, although never on the scale of its neighbours further south along the Fife coast.

Golf started to increase in popularity before the middle of the 19th century; the Royal and Ancient Golf Club adopted its name in the 1830s.

From then onwards the name of St Andrews would forever be synonymous with the sport. Indeed, the manufacture of golf clubs and golf balls were once the only manufacturing industries in the 19th century town.

CRAIL

left: *Shoregate, Crail, c.1906. This narrow wynd sloped down towards the harbour and the Victorian gas works which sat precariously at the edge of the beach just to the right of the harbour. Crail has one of the most picturesque little harbours in Scotland, part of which was built by Robert Stephenson. In Victorian times it supported its own small inshore fishing fleet, but Crail boats never ventured very far from home.*

below: *Market Gate, Crail, as it looked in 1904: a scene which has changed very little in the century since this photograph was taken.*

left: *Every photographer since photography was invented has probably taken this classic view of Crail Harbour. This one dates from c.1902, and like so many other fine early cards was printed in Saxony. The gas works chimney can be seen at the extreme left of the picture.*

Crail has been known as an inshore fishing port for centuries and its little harbour was also used for small-scale export of locally produced goods. By the last decades of the 19th century, it was also starting to attract holidaymakers. "But the dawn of a brighter day has broken upon Crail" wrote D Hay Fleming in his 1886 *Guide to the East Neuk of Fife*, "and when it is better known as a watering place, it will be more highly prized".

He had obviously done his research, and knew the ambitious construction project which was already underway. By the following year Crail had joined the railway age when the Anstruther and St Andrews Railway opened for business on 31st May, and the small railway station opened on the edge of the town. Throughout the 1890s, the popularity of the village as a holiday destination grew, and ultimately led to the establishment of a number of boarding houses and hotels. The railway, rarely (if ever) profitable, survived into the 1960s.

ANSTRUTHER

The church visible on the skyline in most old photographs of Anstruther, Chalmers Free Presbyterian Church, recalls one of Anstruther's most famous sons. The Reverend Dr Thomas Chalmers was one of the founders of the Free Church of Scotland which, at the time of the Disruption in 1843, ceded from the Church of Scotland. The church was demolished in 1991.

"Anstruther", reported Westwood's *Parochial Directory* in 1862, "is one of the best fishing stations in Scotland, and fish-curing is the staple trade of the district. There are also 2 rope and sail factories, 3 oil, and 4 oilskin and fishing-gear factories, a brewery and a tannery. There is also a considerable amount of business done in the export of grain, potatoes etc. Several coasters belong to the port, and a steam-boat plies three times a week to Leith, conveying grain, fish etc., and returning with merchants' goods."

Originally two separate burghs (Easter and Wester Anstruther), the 19th century harbour was also home to Fife's major herring fleet and a major local employer. The history of the industry is celebrated today in the town's award-winning Scottish Fisheries Museum.

The burgh had its own lifeboat from 1865: an open rowing boat which required a crew of twelve.

above: Chalmers Lighthouse and Anstruther Harbour photographed in 1903 by one of James Valentine's photographers. The postcard remained on sale for over 20 years, by which time the children seen here fishing from the quay were probably bringing their own families to enjoy the same pursuit! The lighthouse was completed in 1880, the centenary of Dr Chalmers' birth.

overleaf: Three steam trawlers in Anstruther harbour in 1908.

ELIE & EARLSFERRY

There was a ferry service from Earlsferry to North Berwick 500 years ago and some sources claim that is the derivation of the name. Others prefer the much more romantic legend that the Earl of Fife was ferried to safety from here to Dunbar while escaping from Macbeth!

The villages of Elie and Earlsferry are linked both administratively and physically; Liberty Street runs through both. Their harbours trace their origins back to before the 16th century, although the fishing industries which once sustained both have long gone. Regular steamer services from Leith and Dunbar were initiated in the 1870s to bring tourists to this part of the Fife coast.

After the railway reached Elie in 1863, the popularity of both villages as holiday resorts increased thanks to excellent beaches and (from 1858) a proliferation of fine golf courses. The great Harry Vardon described the Elie course in 1899 as "the best little course I ever played".

LEVEN & METHIL

In the first half of the 20th century, with coal mining in the Fife coalfield at its peak, Methil Docks was the biggest and busiest port on the coast of the county. However, before 1887 when the first dock was opened, Methil was just a small fishing port with a small harbour. Along with nearby Buckhaven to the south, Methil offered one of many safe havens for the fishermen of the Firth of Forth.

The docks were initially developed simply to ship coal from the many collieries in the area. The docks' owners negotiated guaranteed tonnages to be shipped from the port before they even embarked on the development of the site.

Within a few years of the opening, the docks and the supporting industrial railway network had been sold to the North British Railway, under whose ownership Methil Docks embarked on a major expansion. By 1900, the old harbour had disappeared to be replaced by No. 2 Dock with a No. 3 Dock following just before the outbreak of the

above: A c.1903 postcard of Methil's No. 2 Dock which opened in 1900. Although built primarily for the shipping of coal, the port also developed a broad-based general cargo trade. Here there is the typical mixture of sail and steam, so common at the time.

right: According to this c.1904 postcard of Methil Docks, published by W. and A.K. Johnston of Edinburgh, "The spacious docks are the most important in the east of Fife, and admit large vessels, mostly engaged in the shipping of coal". The card was posted in Methil to an address is Liege, Belgium, in June 1908.

Great War, by which time it was one of the country's major coal ports.

In the late 19th century, the contrast between the industrial bustle of Methil and the peaceful holiday ambience of Leven to the north must have been considerable. However, both centres owed their success to the advent of the railway in the 1850s. It was in 1854 that the East Fife Railway opened, linking the coast with Thornton Junction and train services to Edinburgh, Glasgow and Central Scotland. It took 9 years to realise the project, and the 1845 prospectus for the railway had outlined the route: "it will pass by or near to Cameron Bridge, Kennoway, Leven, Largo, Kirkton of Largo, Newburn, Colinsburgh, Kilconquhar, Earls Ferry, Elie, St. Monance, Pittenweem, and terminate at the Harbour of Anstruther". Mineral railways brought the coal to Methil Docks, while the passenger railway brought the tourists to Leven's beautiful beaches.

Leven's expansion, however, came after the Great War. Well into Edwardian times, it was little more than a village despite its growing popularity,

above: A view of Leven High Street from a postcard mailed in 1907, showing the Reform Cooperative Society on the left and Husband's Family Chemists on the right. Husband's had opened for business in 1903. A single deck electric tram approaches. Trams had been introduced into the town by the Wemyss and District Tramway Company Ltd in August 1906, so this postcard would have been among the first to feature them.

left: Boys sailing model yachts in the Scoonie Burn, Leven, c.1908, near where the burn was crossed by the railway around the Fife coast.

A timeless view of Dysart, taken in the 1890s, and published as a postcard c.1903. Dysart's prosperity can be traced back to mediaeval times, and it had a considerable trade for the export of coal and salt. Linen manufacture had all but died out by Victorian times but, like nearby Kirkcaldy, Victorian Dysart was a centre for canvas manufacture. The crow-stepped gables of the 18th century buildings led some locals to describe the Pan Ha' area of the town as Little Holland.

DYSART

Dysart may today officially be part of Kirkcaldy (the two burghs merged in 1930), but in Victorian and Edwardian times it proudly held on to its individuality. Indeed, in the 17th century, it had seen Kirkcaldy as a considerable rival to its salt trade and its harbour. Trade started to deteriorate in the 18th century, prompting Daniel Defoe in 1726 (in his *Journey Through the Whole Island of Great Britain*) to describe it as "a most lamentable object of a miserable, dying corporation".

Despite some improvement in fortune in the early 19th century, Victorian Dysart was still considered by many to be a town in decline. Francis Groome's *Ordnance Gazetteer of Scotland* published in the 1880s devoted some extensive space to its history and the crow-stepped gable houses which had dominated the waterfront for 200 years, but commented that "the harbour, comprising an outer basin and an inner wet-dock (once a quarry) with 18 feet of water and berthage for 17 or 18 vessels, is ample enough for all the scant commerce Dysart still retains".

Once having enjoyed a significant export trade in salt and coal, the harbour was by then too small for most of the ships which exported coal from the Fife coalfields. Indeed, much coal trade had been lost to Methil when the harbour was closed for some time to be dredged. Despite the deepened harbour being capable to taking ships up to 400 tons, much of that trade did not return.

Dysart's collieries, however – the underground roads for which ran thousands of yards under the Firth of Forth – still delivered coal to the ships at the quayside in Edwardian times via a mineral railway. They also dumped much of their spoil into the sea, a practice which proved detrimental to the town developing itself as a resort.

The Harbour head, Kirkcaldy, 1906. The steamer John Strachan – seen loading at the left – was built in 1885 for the Kirkcaldy Leith and Glasgow Steam Packet Company, and had a gross tonnage of 73 tons. The port was tidal until the mid 1840s, when the new harbour was built at a cost of £40,000

'The Bucket Pats' on Kirkcaldy beach in 1903

KIRKCALDY

Kirkcaldy expanded at a rate through the 18th and 19th centuries which was unprecedented in its long history. By 1900 it was a thriving industrial community, employing large numbers of people in manufacturing, ceramics, coal mining, ship-building and import and export.

Power loom weaving (of both linen and canvas) was introduced to Scotland in Kirkcaldy in the early 1800s, but it was the use of that canvas in the floorcloth manufacturing industry with which the name of Kirkcaldy became synonymous. The town grew into the world's largest producer of floor coverings. From the first oil-cloth factory which opened in 1847 (built by Michael Nairn, a Dundee-trained jute weaver) and through the introduction of linoleum manufacture in 1877, the industry grew exponentially well into the 20th century.

Due to the all-pervading odour of boiling linseed oil, a basic ingredient in linoleum manufacture, it was often said that you could smell Kirkcaldy from the train long before you could see it!

above: This delightful view, entitled 'Feeding the Swans, Beveridge Park Lake, Kirkcaldy' is one of quite a large number of postcards of the park which were available in the first decade of last century. Published by Hartmann, c.1903, it was printed in Saxony.

left: Kirkcaldy's High Street in 1904. Electric street lighting had been introduced 2 years earlier in 1902, and the trams had been introduced in February 1903. Kirkcaldy Corporation Tramways reportedly carried half a million passengers in the first three months — more than twelve times the burgh's total population!

ABERDOUR & BURNTISLAND

Aberdour's 18th century Stone Pier was constructed to increase the quantity of coal which could be exported from the small port; the Fife coalfield was itself going through a major expansion. The coal business was relatively short-lived however and, by the mid 1850s, most of the vessels using the pier were pleasure steamers running regular services to and from Leith. The coal traffic largely migrated to the bigger harbour at nearby Burntisland which also handled a range of heavy cargos, had shipbuilding facilities and several major industries. Today Burntisland's industrial heritage is largely history, the town seeking to attract tourists.

By the end of the century, an extension to Aberdour pier had been constructed especially for the tourist traffic, and a wooden pier built to handle steamers at low tide.

By the 1890s the village had been connected to Edinburgh by railway with the opening of the line from the Forth Bridge. It snaked around the Fife coast connecting Aberdour with Burntisland, Kirkcaldy and Leven to the east. At Burntisland, the line separated the town from the beach.

Aberdour owes its existence to the 14th century castle, the ruins of which still dominate the place. When the railway arrived, it cut a swathe through the ancient approach to the castle; in Victorian times, antiquities were not treated with the respect they warrant today.

Aberdour stands either side of the mouth of the Dour Burn and was originally known by two separate names of Easter and Wester Aberdour. The mouth of the burn was the first harbour.

While Aberdour remained a relatively quiet village, Burntisland had expanded considerably by 1900. It continued to do so in the first half of the 20th century, with aluminium smelting adding to its range of industries and to traffic in the harbour.

On an island in the Firth of Forth, opposite Aberdour, stand the magnificent ruins of the 13th century Inchcolm Abbey. Until the current ferry service from South Queensferry slipway was initiated in the 1980s, access to the abbey was reached by open boat from Aberdour sands.

opposite page top: *Shore Road, Aberdour in 1903. Kinnairds Tea Gardens advertised 'Picnics and Excursions Purveyed for Any Numbers' and that it had Ladies Rooms!*

middle: *The High Street, Aberdour, from a Valentine's Series postcard mailed in 1904 to an address in Singapore. The postal cost was just one old penny.*

bottom: *Also from Valentine's, this animated 1907 postcard shows the view across the water towards the beach at Burntisland, the town's industrial quarter well out of sight.*

this page above: *The Stone Pier, Aberdour, from a postcard c.1909. The paddle steamer is probably the 277 ton* Redgauntlet. *Built in 1895, she spent much of her working life on the Clyde before transferring to service on the Forth in 1909. She continued to work on the Forth until the outbreak of the First World War.*

left: *The busy beach at Burntisland, depicted in a Valentines Series postcard c.1905. At the top left, a train can be seen making its way towards Kinghorn and Kirkcaldy along the Fife coast.*

above: The 1879 paddle steamer William Muir *photographed at Burntisland, c.1901, and published as a 'Reliable Series' postcard after 1902. This card was posted in Burntisland in March 1908. Later re-engined with a single funnel and 50 tons heavier, she served the route until 1917 and then again from 1919 until 1937.*

Until 1890, rail passengers for the north of Scotland usually travelled by train from Edinburgh to Granton, transferred to a ferry, then back to the train again at Burntisland. The 364 ton 1879-built *William Muir* spent over 50 years carrying passengers across the estuary between Edinburgh and Fife, except for a hiatus during the Great War. Then, like so many other coastal paddle-steamers, she served as a minesweeper in the Thames estuary. *William Muir* and her sister-ship *John Stirling* were both named after directors of the North British Railway who operated the service.

After the opening of the Forth Bridge in 1890, the NBR disposed of most of its steamers but retained *William Muir*. Initially designed for carrying passengers and horses, she was extensively rebuilt in 1910 to carry vehicles as well. After 1890, *John Stirling* saw service on the south coast and on the Manchester Ship Canal.

William Muir earned a unique if somewhat macabre place in Scotland's history when she was involved in the aftermath of the collapse of the first Tay Bridge in late December 1879, bringing the bodies back to Burntisland.

SOUTH QUEENSFERRY

The little village of South Queensferry takes its name from the Queen's ferry established by the monks of Dunfermline Abbey at the instigation of Queen Margaret, the wife of King Malcolm III, in the 11th century.

For centuries thereafter, the ferry carried pilgrims making their way from Edinburgh to Dunfermline and then north to St Andrews. They embarked from and returned to various points close to the village; the actual landing place was dependent upon the tides and the weather. From rowing boat to steamer, the ferry operated for nearly 900 years until the opening of the Forth Road Bridge in 1964.

Queensferry was a thriving port by the 17th century, exporting a variety of goods to mainland Europe including coal and wool. Its successful shop owners and merchants built many of the fine houses which still give the village so much of its character. From the 17th century, travellers could rest and eat at the Hawes Inn near the ferry slipway, a location immortalised in *Kidnapped* by Robert Louis Stevenson.

By the 19th century, Queensferry's importance as a port was in decline but fishing was a growing source of wealth and employment. Soap and linen manufacture had been introduced to the village and, but for the arrival of the railway, Queensferry might have remained no more than a small port on the Firth of Forth.

The decision to bridge the river between South and North Queensferry – talked about throughout the century – was finally taken in the early 1870s and the Forth Bridge Company was incorporated in 1873. A foundation stone was laid in the same year, but the original bridge (designed by Thomas Bouch) would never be built. Bouch lost the contract when his Tay Bridge collapsed in 1879.

Work on the eventual design started in 1882, and the bridge grew steadily over the following 8 years. It was opened with great pomp and ceremony by the Prince of Wales (later King Edward VII) on 4th March 1890 when the Prince drove home the last ceremonial rivet.

Despite the fact that the bridge became an instant

top: South Queensferry High Street from the east, a postcard by James Valentine of Dundee c.1908.

above: Overshadowed by the viaducts for the bridge, a coach draws up at the Hawes Inn. A Valentine postcard c.1905.

The ferry Forfarshire *arriving at South Queensferry slipway, c.1908. Built in 1861,* Forfarshire *spent more than 30 years on the River Tay, plying between Newport-on-Tay and Dundee, before moving to the Forth in 1893. She was fitted with the tall funnel seen here during a major refit in 1904, and continued to work the river until scrapped in 1922.*

tourist attraction, eminent critics such as John Ruskin remained convinced it was "the supremest specimen of all ugliness", while others thought that its complex and functional geometric structure would have been improved with a bit of ornament!

George Washington Wilson and James Valentine photographed every stage of its construction, and their photographs proved popular with the many visitors who came to inspect progress. Others came from all over the world to photograph the bridge in its complete state; many still do today.

The images taken by the official photographer, Evelyn Carey, provide a priceless record of this enormous undertaking using the tiny figures of the workers to underline the huge scale of the project.

Ferries continued to cross the river on a course parallel to the bridge, affording splendid views of what was described as the greatest engineering feat of the Victorian age. Anyone from South Queensferry wishing to cross the river by train had to travel first to Dalmeny Station a couple of miles away.

top: A train arriving at Dalmeny Station in 1906. Beyond it, the south tower of the bridge can be seen in the distance. Today nearly 200 trains, some weighing over 1500 tons, still use the bridge daily.

above: American photographers Strohmeyer and Wyman took an extensive series of stereoscopic (3D) views of the Forth Bridge in 1895/96, which were marketed both by them and by Underwood and Underwood.

left: A Valentine view of the site in 1886 shows the three towers at different stages in their construction.

113

above left: Edwardian fisherwomen, from a postcard c.1904, carried on the tradition of posing for the camera which could be traced back to the earliest days of photography in Scotland. Whereas the earliest photographers had taken their pictures on location in Newhaven, these women had been paid to visit an Edinburgh studio.

right: A postcard from c.1907 of fisherfolk, Newhaven, presents a much more idyllic view of the fishing quarter than A W Hill's 'Slum' (far right). Neither was strictly accurate, although living conditions in the fishermen's cottages was never especially comfortable. Many of these houses had been built during the village's expansion in the 17th and 18th centuries.

114

NEWHAVEN

The fishing community in the port of Newhaven was among the first in Scotland to be captured by the camera.

In 1845, the pioneer Scottish photographers David Octavius Hill and Robert Adamson visited the village on several occasions, producing a remarkable series of images of the fishermen and women at their work.

In its infancy, photography was a very slow and cumbersome process, requiring the subjects to stay absolutely still for the duration of the long exposure. The subjects were therefore often posed to give them a firm support against which to rest or lean.

Interest in photographs of the fisherwomen and their creels was considerable and continued into the postcard era, with the women being taken to Edinburgh studios to pose against 'coastal' backdrops. The women were not unwilling to make the journey into the city, as there was invariably a small fee for their trouble!

Lying between Granton and Leith, Newhaven got its name in the early 16th century when it became the royal dockyard for James IV's navy, replacing their old haven further up the Firth of Forth next to Blackness Castle.

By the 19th century Newhaven was one of the east coast's major herring ports and the fisherwives were a familiar sight on the streets of Edinburgh selling the fish from their creels, calling out 'caller herring' as they went. They were proud of their voices and, in the 19th century, established a fisherwomen's choir. The choir was still going strong a century later, the women performing both at home and abroad wearing the traditional working dress of their predecessors.

above right: New Lane, Newhaven, 1906; an animated scene in a narrow lane running down to the shore.

right: From the camera of amateur photographer Alexander Wilson Hill, c.1910, this study is titled 'A Slum' and captures a corner of Newhaven's harbour district and the sort of housing available to the Edwardian fisherfolk. Despite the pejorative title, Hill's bromoil transfer print romanticises the poor housing and hardly even hints at the hardship which went with living conditions like these.

LEITH & EDINBURGH

main picture: *This romantic picture of a steam tug in Leith Docks was taken c.1910 by the eminent amateur photographer Alexander Wilson Hill who had, at the time, just been promoted to the headquarters of the Commercial Bank of Scotland in Edinburgh.*

inset: *The Sailors' Home, Leith Docks, looking past the funnel and paddle box of the same steamer from a 1905 St Giles Series postcard mailed to an Edinburgh address.*

The port of Leith, the pre-eminent port on Scotland's east coast for centuries, is today a shadow of its former self.

While the area has been and is undergoing an extensive and inspiring redevelopment, the glory days of the port are long past.

Edinburgh's port has a history going back at least 900 years and, until the middle of the 19th century when it was overtaken by Glasgow, it was the country's most important trading outlet. Its quays were piled high with timber, iron and a wide variety of perishable goods. Nearby shipbuilding and dry dock facilities were the town's most important employers.

The eminent engineer, John Rennie, started work in 1799 on designing the extensive docks which replaced the older and much smaller quays on which the port had depended for centuries.

Leith's sand bar was the major obstacle to the port's expansion, restricting the size of ships which could gain access to the docks. Rennie's design partially overcame the problems of the encroaching sand, and his design envisaged three large docks extending almost as far as Newhaven. The final part of his grand plan was never carried out however, but between 1802 and 1817 the east and west docks were created. Neither of these still exists.

In the middle of the 19th century, the port underwent a period of massive expansion which increased its capacity several-fold.

The Victoria Dock was opened in 1851, the Prince of Wales Graving Dock in 1863 and the Albert Dock in 1869. The Edinburgh Dock followed in 1881 and the huge Imperial Dock in 1904.

Further huge expansion between the wars turned Leith into a major world-class port, but changing circumstances eventually proved to be its limitation. The increasing size of much modern shipping, coupled with the depth restrictions which have always plagued Leith, signalled the port's decline; shipbuilding ceased in the 1980s.

In 2004, Forth Ports announced their intention to completely close the docks and develop the area for housing and mixed usage.

The area is now being extensively redeveloped as a fashionable suburb of Edinburgh. Despite the fact that Leith is now part of Edinburgh, centuries of

above: James Valentine's studio produced this view of the new Imperial Dock just after it was opened in 1904. The steamers Iona, Wrecker and a third unidentified ship dominate the picture.

below: The Sailors' Home and Tower, Leith Docks, from a 1907 postcard. The 1885 Sailors Home became the Angel Hotel, and the round tower was originally a 17th century windmill!

below: In this 1904 postcard view of Leith's 'New Dock' (more correctly known as the Imperial Dock and opened in the year this picture was taken) a mixture of sail and steam, typical of the period, can be seen. Among the ships are vessels registered in Leith, Liverpool and, on the left, the sailing ship Lina *registered in Kragero, Norway. To the right is what appears to be a 19th century warship.*

rivalry between them led to considerable resistance to its incorporation within the city.

When King Robert I granted the harbour of Leith to the city of Edinburgh in 1329, the city magistrates passed a regulation forbidding the construction of streets within the burgh large enough to allow a cart to pass through: a strange decision for a port! The town was therefore developed with more than its fair share of narrow vennels and wynds built around the Water of Leith, a layout which changed little over the following centuries.

At its peak, Leith had a population of over 80,000 people many of whom worked somewhere within the hundred acres of dockland or in the industries which surrounded the docks. These included shipbuilding, whisky distilling, soap making, sail making, rope making and engineering.

In the early 20th century, Leith was Britain's second most important port exporting to America, Canada, Japan and the Far East, as well as to the many ports on the western seaboard of Europe. Ships from long-forgotten lines such as the Leith, Hull and Hamburgh Steam Packet Company were the lifeblood of the port.

A huge crowd on board the paddle steamer Wemyss Castle as she prepares to leave the West Pier at Leith c.1903. The card was posted to an address in Leytonstone, to remind the recipient of a summer holiday outing in July 1905. The 172 ton steamer had been built in Port Glasgow on the DC Gareloch in 1872 for service on the Gare Loch working out of Craigendoran and Helensburgh. She was renamed in 1891 when ownership was transferred from the North British Steam Packet Company to the Galloway Saloon Steam Packet Company. She regularly sailed from Leith to North Berwick and round the Fife coast calling at Aberdour, Elie, Anstruther and elsewhere.

A large crowd watching a match in progress on the Bowling Green on Leith Links, c.1909. The card was published by Valentine.

above: Princes Street Gardens and the Royal Mile during a concert at the bandstand in 1904. The gardens were created in the 18th century, on the site of the Nor' Loch. This was drained when the New Town was built. Between the gardens and the castle rock, the railway tracks run through cuttings and tunnels towards Waverly Station.

below: The Royal Procession making its way to the Palace of Holyroodhouse on the occasion of the visit of King Edward VII and Queen Alexandra in May 1903, their first visit to Scotland since the Coronation the previous year. The streets of Edinburgh along their route were decked with bunting and ceremonial arches. Edward was no stranger to Scotland's capital, having lived and studied in the city for a period while a young man.

The port of Leith grew up to serve Scotland's capital, and although not, itself, by the sea, Edinburgh warrants a mention in this book by virtue of its history and its importance.

Although Edinburgh and Leith have grown together, they retain their own identities, albeit with leith forever in the shadow of its neighbour.

Late 19th and early 20th century Edinburgh had to cope with two vividly constrasting descriptions: to some it was 'the Athens of the North' and to others 'Auld Reekie'. The former suggests a city of great architectural beauty but the latter a place where smoke pollution was a constant and major problem; both were true.

It was to that city that George IV arrived in 1822 to take part in a series of events stage-managed by Sir Walter Scott. These events, among others, led to a massive increase in interest in the Scottish clans and to the introduction of many of the clan tartans which figure so heavily in Scottish tradition today.

In Queen Victoria's day, it was very much a city of two halves. The Georgian 'New Town' with its wide streets was a model of fine living, while the mediaeval tenements of the old town were increasingly unsafe and unhealthy. Indeed, if one did not die from the diseases which rampaged through the dark alleyways, there was always the risk of the buildings themselves collapsing. One such incident occurred in November 1861, when two tenements on the High Street fell down killing 35 people. The replacement tenement became known as 'Heave Awa' Hoose' after, according to a story of the time, a plaintiff cry was heard from one of the men buried under the rubble, exhorting his rescuers to "Heave awa' lad, I'm no deid yet!"

Such collapses prompted Lord Provost William Chambers to initiate a major improvement scheme in 1866 (at the same time as a similar project was sweeping away much of Glasgow's mediaeval slums). Many of the worst buildings were demolished to be replaced with slightly lower-density housing.

Many buildings were demolished only to street level, and the Victorian tenements built over the top of the 16th and 17th century remains. The older closes and wynds survive to this day – a labyrinth of subterranean passageways and buildings largely hidden from view and forgotten.

The dividing line between the mediaeval city and the Georgian New Town was marked by that most Victorian of inventions: the railway tracks which ran below the castle rock from Haymarket to Waverly station. Waverly was built by the North British Railway in the 1860s on the sites of three earlier stations. The Caledonian Railway opened its first station in Lothian Road in 1848. The great Princes Street Station at the West End was completed in 1890 but the adjoining Caledonian Hotel – all that remains of the station today – was not completed until 1903.

Much of Princes Street (as well as the small streets between Princes Street and George Street) dates from the second half of the 19th century when many of the elegant shop frontages were erected. That reconstruction continued into the 20th century, when some rather ill-considered designs were inflicted on the city's premier shopping street!

The history of photography in Scotland is firmly rooted in Edinburgh, with the pioneering work of David Octavius Hill and Robert Adamson. They took the photographs used as reference for Hill's giant painting of the 'Signing of the Deed of Demission at Tanfield in 1843', which marked the cessation of the Free Church from the Church of Scotland.

above left: The Edinburgh skyline as seen from the castle in 1897 – reminding us how close it is to the sea.

above: The city's premier shopping street, Princes Street, one of many such postcards available in 1904,

below: A small crowd of onlookers watch the Argyll & Sutherland Highlanders on parade on the Esplanade at Edinburgh Castle in 1902. Military parades have been popular subjects since the 19th century.

PORTOBELLO & JOPPA

Before Portobello was developed, the people of Edinburgh promenaded along Seafield Beach closer to the city. The early-Victorian expansion of Leith Docks put paid to Seafield as a resort, however, and the capital's citizens moved further east for their pleasure. That stretch of coastline was acquired by the Leith Docks Company in 1806 and Seafield's fashionable sands rapidly disappeared beneath the industrial sprawl of the docklands.

Portobello was a small village developed around a cottage built by a sailor called George Hamilton, named after a famous 18th century naval victory against the Spanish at Puerto Bello. It already had a popular beach before the end of the 1790s, complete with "bathing-machines upon the best construction, with sturdy horses and careful drivers" and by the early 19th century its popularity was growing.

According to Groome's *Ordnance Gazetteer* in 1804, "the fineness of its sands, and its general eligibility as a bathing place, began to draw the attention of the City of Edinburgh, converting the town into a fashionable watering place".

Hot and cold seawater baths (an essential facility for every self-respecting resort) opened in 1806. This was the same year that a thrice-daily horse-drawn coach service was introduced, linking the town with Edinburgh.

Trains arrived in 1846 when the North British Railway reached the town. The popularity of the resort was considerable by the end of the century, drawing holidaymakers from all over Scotland. So

above: This romantic picture of Portobello's bathing beach was taken in the early years of the 20th century, one of a huge assortment of postcards on sale in this popular tourist resort.

left: Posted in 1906, and taken in 1905, the crowded beach attests to the resort's popularity. Its close proximity to Edinburgh made Portobello the ideal destination for a day out despite the fact that, at high tide, the beach was reduced to a relatively narrow strip of crowded sand.

far left: An animated scene on Portobello Beach in 1904 or 1905. Posted by Meg to her friend 'Miss Bryce' on 10th July 1906, the message confirmed that the weather was every bit as good as shown in the photograph!

great was the demand for rail travel that Portobello station boasted the longest platform on any suburban station in Scotland.

To cater for the huge influx of visitors there was a funfair, a magnificent seawater bathing pool, Thomas Bouch's pier and rows of houses offering holiday accommodation at a variety of prices. However, as people's holiday expectations grew to more than a short tram or train journey from Edinburgh, the resort's light rather faded.

Bouch's pier was demolished in 1917, the funfair and the railway are both long gone, and Portobello is now a quiet suburb of Edinburgh.

top right: Looking east down Portobello's High Street, c.1908.

centre: On Portobello Pier in the closing years of the 19th century. In addition to advertisements for tea, Oxo and a host of other essential products including Singer Sewing Machines, posters advertise steamer trips to the nearby Bass Rock, the Isle of May and North Berwick as well as ferry crossings to the Fife towns of Elie and Methil. This photograph, taken in 1899, was first used on a coloured postcard c.1908. Compared with many of England's piers, this was a very simple affair, with little shelter from the east coast winds.

below right: Portobello Pier c.1909. The Portobello Pier Company was established in the late 1860s, and the pier opened in 1871. Built at a cost of ten thousand pounds, the pier was 1250 feet in length, with the essential pavilion at the sea end. It was designed by Thomas Bouch, later to achieve infamy as the designer-engineer of the ill-fated first Tay Bridge. The pier, however, survived longer than the bridge, eventually being demolished in 1917.

below: Portobello Bathing Beach as seen from the pier walkway in a 1906 postcard, again from a Victorian negative.

left: The passengers on an early motor omnibus watch as one of Musselburgh's electric trams passes an Edinburgh cable tram in Joppa in 1905. At that point, passengers travelling to Musselburgh had to change from one tram system to the other. The cable tram is standing at the eastern terminus of the Edinburgh system; there are only tracks for the electric system running in the foreground of the photograph. Edinburgh's cable tramway was one of the most extensive ever built, and survived into the 1920s when the system was electrified. Three-inch diameter cables or chains ran at a constant speed in slots down the centre of the roadway, powered from engine houses at various points along each route. The longest cable measured six and a half miles! To start the tram, the driver dropped a gripper beneath the tram into the slot and grabbed the moving cable. When the car approached a stop, the cable was disengaged and the tram free-wheeled until the brakes were applied. Freewheeling was also necessary when switching from one cable to another. Introduced in 1899 to replace the city's horse-drawn trams it was, in fact, ideally suited to the capital's hilly terrain. The flatter routes of the Musselburgh cars, however, proved no problem for available electric tram technology. The electric route from Musselburgh had reached Joppa at the end of 1902, only a year after cable trams had been introduced on the route from Joppa to Leith.

left: This view over the rooftops of Joppa towards Portobello Pier was published by Flockhart of Joppa c.1903. The tramcar is standing at the cable terminus, and at the same point as it is in the upper picture.

MUSSELBURGH

Musselburgh lies on the east bank of the River Esk, six miles east of Edinburgh, with the village and harbour of Fisherrow on the west. The town's name dates back 8 centuries to the discovery of a mussel bank in the Esk estuary; the settlement was originally known as Eskmouth.

The town of Musselburgh claims to be the oldest in Scotland, tracing its origins back to the Romans who in 80 AD built a fort on the banks of the river and a bridge which once spanned it. The foundations of that bridge are said to still support part of the Old Bridge which can trace its own history back to the 13th century. The New Bridge was built by the eminent engineer John Rennie in 1807.

Throughout the 19th century, fishing remained an important source of employment. The town later diversified into a variety of manufacturing industries. By the early 20th century, with an efficient electric tram service which was introduced in 1904 (19 years before Edinburgh electrified its service), the number of people commuting to the capital 6 miles away started to increase.

The town has a strong sporting tradition. It has enjoyed its famous racecourse on the links since the early 19th century, where both flat racing and steeplechasing meetings are held.

The links also have strong historical ties with golf. Indeed, it was in Musselburgh that the world's first 'championship' golf match for women took place in 1811 when local fisherwives played for a unique trophy: a Creel and Skull. Sixty-three years later, in the golf course's centenary year of 1874, the Open was held at Musselburgh for the first of six times. In the following decade, local golfer Bob Ferguson won the championship three times on that same course.

The Open, first held in Prestwick in 1860, was moved to St Andrews in 1873 and then Musselburgh in the following year. Those three venues alternated until 1889. In those days, golfers played with hickory-shafted clubs and gutta-percha balls. Modern-day golfers can still experience (and perhaps even enjoy) this challenge as old-style equipment is available for hire.

top: A tram for Portobello passing the Tolbooth in 1904.

above: At the opposite end of the High Street, a horse and cart is seen passing an open decked tram in this 1905 view.

right: An earlier view of the High Street in 1902 before the tram lines and overhead cables were installed.

COCKENZIE & PORT SETON

Cockenzie harbour was the terminus of the first working railway in Scotland. A horse-drawn tramway was opened in 1722 to carry coal from Tranent colliery, so the harbour had been industrialised more than a century before Queen Victoria came to the throne.

Like many small coal ports, it was also involved in both salt making and boat building.

Port Seton, where salt was also manufactured until the end of the 19th century, had developed as a fishing village and still retains an inshore fleet today. Facilities at both harbours continued to be developed throughout the 19th century.

By the second half of the 19th century, with ease of travel from Edinburgh, Port Seton had started to reinvent itself as a holiday resort.

below: A crowd of locals and holidaymakers at Port Seton bartering with the fisherfolk at the daily fish market held on the beach. This 'Ingle Series' card, posted to Bath in December 1905, was photographed and published by Alex Inglis of Calton Hill, Edinburgh.

NORTH BERWICK

North Berwick was "A fishing village with drying nets, scolding wives, the smell of fish and seaweed and the blowing sands" according to Robert Louis Stevenson in 1888, describing his regular childhood holiday destination.

Ever since the introduction of statutory holidays, the idea of visiting the miles of beautiful sandy coastline southeast of Edinburgh has been popular. North Berwick as a holiday destination therefore has a long tradition, considerably enhanced by the North British Railway Company's introduction of a single-track railway service as early as 1849. The gradient of the track, however, proved too great for the rudimentary locomotives introduced by the company. For six months in 1856, steam was replaced by horse drawn 'Dandy Cars' on the line until more powerful locomotives could be sourced.

The town enjoyed considerable amenities in the mid 19th century. A gas works opened in 1845, ensuring that North Berwick's streets were illuminated until 10.30 pm (when, as all good people should be abed by then, the twenty gas lamps were switched off). A telegraph office opened in the High Street in 1870, the first in East Lothian, giving the town almost instantaneous access to the rest of the world.

Despite all these technological advances, North Berwick's resident population remained under one thousand until almost the end of the 19th century. Records tell of over three thousand visitors regularly staying in the town at any time during the late Victorian summer season, however.

Like most east coast resorts, golf was and still is a major attraction. The town's courses were among the finest in Scotland. In 1899 one professional tournament brought over nine thousand spectators by rail in a single day to watch the proceedings (a far cry from the 1850s, when closing the railway was a real possibility as it was losing so much money!)

The days when North Berwick advertised itself as the 'Biarritz of the North' and attracted the cream of English and Scottish society to its hotels and holiday homes may have long gone, but the little town still has much to offer.

top: *Work on the Bathing Pond started in 1899, being completed in time for summer 1900.*

above: *The delightfully named Quality Street, as it was c.1902.*

right: *North Berwick beach, 1903, posted to a friend in Edinburgh by a golfing holidaymaker who wrote "I have been on the links all morning - really it is a beautiful day!"*

DUNBAR

Looking at the relatively few fishing boats in the harbour at Dunbar today, it is hard to imagine the place crammed with hundreds of craft in the 18th and 19th century when it was one of the most important herring-fishing ports on the southeast coast of Scotland.

The town's close-knit fishing community lived around the harbour in narrow streets and alleys. The men crewed the herring boats and their womenfolk gutted the catch on the quayside when they returned.

As in so many small fishing ports, the gradual disappearance of the herring during the second half of the 19th century caused considerable hardship. Some fishermen adapted and changed (fishing for shellfish instead of herring) and their successors still fish out of the small harbour today.

above: A small fishing boat leaving Dunbar's Victoria Harbour (also known as New Harbour) in 1906, passing beneath the ruins of the town's ancient castle. The new harbour had been completed in 1842.

right: Cat's Row, Dunbar, c1905, was home to many members of the town's fishing community. Like fishermen's quarters in most small ports, it ran down towards the harbour. Today it is known as Victoria Street. Dunbar had been a successful herring fishing port since the early 18th century but, by the time this photograph was taken, the fishing industry was in dramatic decline.

EYEMOUTH

Eyemouth once supported a highly successful herring industry as well as a busy commercial port. In 1804, the *Gazetteer of Scotland* described Eyemouth as "A considerable town and parish in the county of Berwick… at the beginning of the last century Eyemouth was a small fishing village, which afforded a retreat for smugglers; but, shortly after the union that pernicious trade being much quashed, the gentlemen of the county took advantage of the excellent natural harbour formed by the river Eye and erected a pier on both sides by voluntary subscription…Population in 1801, 899."

On October 14th 1881, known locally as 'Disaster Day' a ferocious storm took the local fishing fleet completely by surprise not long after they had left port. At least 40 vessels were at sea when the storm broke, and only 26 made it back to port. The loss of life – 129 men – amounted to more than one-third of the town's fishermen.

The harbour was constructed in the late 18th century and subsequently enlarged on several occasions. Seen here in a view published in 1902 but probably taken in the 1890s, the quay is lined by a mixture of fishing boats and small cargo vessels.

INDEX